Translated from the French by Lionel Abel

The Documents of Modern Art: vol. 1.

The Cubist Painters

Aesthetic Meditations 1913

Guillaume Apollinaire

George Wittenborn, Inc. New York, 1962

Editor's Note: In typography and illustrative matter the present
edition is greatly changed from the edition of 1944, the first
volume to appear in this series. The translation by Lionel Abel
of Apollinaire's poetic text remains unaltered, but a long,
characteristic poem by Apollinaire and a detailed bibliography have
been added; the small, documentary illustrations of cubist
works of the original edition have been replaced by larger illustrations
having to do with Apollinaire himself.

Publisher's Note: The publisher of this series
wishes to express his gratitude and indebtedness to all those
who have given him advice and assistance, especially to Mr.
Roger Shattuck and "Yale French Studies" for permission to reproduce
his translation of a poem by Apollinaire; and Librairie Gallimard
for reproduction of the original. He hopes that he has not
infringed on anybody's copyrighted material in selecting literary
quotations or illustrative material.

Manufactured in the United States of America
by E. L. Hildreth & Co., Brattleboro, Vermont
Offset reprint, 1962, manufactured by
Speed-O-Lite Offset Co., New York, N. Y.

This is the first volume in the series,
"The Documents of Modern Art".

Cover design and typography by Paul Rand

Contents:

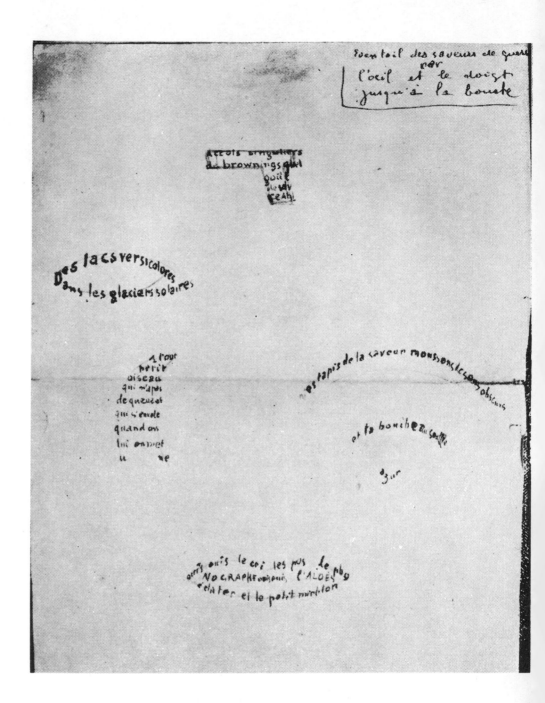

L'ÉCRITURE DE 1915.
Des lacs versicolores.

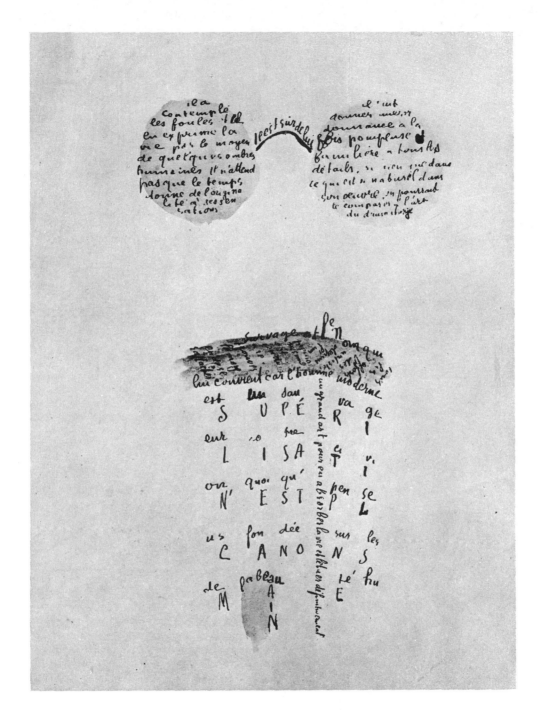

L'ÉCRITURE DE 1917.
Pour Léopold Survage.

List of Illustrations:

Phantom of the Clouds

Phantom of the Clouds

It was the day before July 14
About four in the afternoon
I went out to see the saltimbanques

Those men who make turns in the air
Are beginning to be rare in Paris
In my youth one saw many more than today
They are almost all gone to the provinces

I took the boulevard Saint-Germain
And on a little square between Saint-Germain-des-Prés and the statue of Danton
I found some saltimbanques
The crowd which surrounded them was silent and resigned to waiting
I found a place in the group where I could see everything

Formidable weights
Whole Belgian cities held up at arm's length by a Russian worker from Longwy
Black hollow dumb-bells with a frozen river for a shaft
Fingers rolling a cigarette as bitter and delicious as life

Several dirty rugs lie on the ground
Rugs with creases that would never come out
Rugs which are almost entirely the color of dust
And where a few yellow and green spots still show
Like a tune which will not leave you

See that thin savage looking one
The ashes of his ancestors are coming out in his grey beard
He carries all his heredity in his face
And seems to dream of the future
While mechanically turning a Barbary hand-organ
Whose sweet voice wails marvellously
Gurgling false notes and muffled groans

The saltimbanques didn't move
The oldest wore tights of that purplish rose color which glows in the cheeks of
    those lively little girls who are near death
That rose nestles most in the wrinkles around their mouths
Or next to their nostrils
It is a color full of treachery

Did that man carry thus around his waist
The vile color of his lungs

Arms arms everywhere mounted guard

The second saltimbanque
Was clothed only in his shadow
I looked long at him

Un Fantôme de Nuées

Comme c'était la veille du quatorze juillet
Vers les quatre heures de l'après-midi
Je descendis dans la rue pour aller voir les saltimbanques

Ces gens qui font des tours en plein air
Commencent à être rares à Paris
Dans ma jeunesse on en voyait beaucoup plus qu'aujourd'hui
Ils s'en sont allés presque tous en province

Je pris le boulevard Saint-Germain
Et sur une petite place située entre Saint-Germain-des-Prés et la statue de Danton
Je rencontrai les saltimbanques
La foule les entourait muette et résignée à attendre
Je me fis une place dans ce cercle afin de tout voir

Poids formidables
Villes de Belgique soulevées à bras tendu par un ouvrier russe de Longwy
Haltères noirs et creux qui ont pour tige un fleuve figé
Doigts roulant une cigarette amère et délicieuse comme la vie

De nombreux tapis sales couvraient le sol
Tapis qui ont des plis qu'on ne défera pas
Tapis qui sont presque entièrement couleur de la poussière
Et où quelques taches jaunes ou vertes ont persisté
Comme un air de musique qui vous poursuit

Vois-tu le personnage maigre et sauvage
La cendre de ses pères lui sortait en barbe grisonnante
Il portait ainsi toute son hérédité au visage
Il semblait rêver à l'avenir
En tournant machinalement un orgue de Barbarie
Dont la lente voix se lamentait merveilleusement
Les glouglous les couacs et les sourds gémissements

Les saltimbanques ne bougeaient pas
Le plus vieux avait un maillot couleur de ce rose violâtre qu'ont aux joues cer-
    taines jeunes filles fraîches mais près de la mort
Ce rose-là se niche surtout dans les plis qui entourent souvent leur bouche
Ou près des narines
C'est un rose plein de traîtrise

Cet homme portait-il ainsi sur le dos
La teinte ignoble de ses poumons

Les bras les bras partout montaient la garde

Le second saltimbanque
N'était vêtu que de son ombre
Je le regardai longtemps

His face escapes me entirely
He was a man without a head

Another one looked like an urchin
A good Apache but debauched
With his comic pants and garters
Getting dressed wouldn't he have looked like a pimp

The music stopped for a parley with the audience
Which tossed the sum of 2 francs 5 sou by sou on the rug
Instead of the 3 francs which the old one had set as the price of a performance

But when it was clear that no one would give anything more
They decided to begin
From behind the organ a small saltimbanque came out dressed in consumptive red
With fur at his wrists and ankles
He gave a few brief cries
And saluted with his forearms prettily held
His hands spread out

With one leg back ready to genuflect
He bowed to the four cardinal points
And when he balanced on a ball
His slim body became so delicate a music that none of the spectators could resist it
A tiny spirit without humanity
Everyone thought
And this music of shapes
Destroyed that of the mechanical organ
Which was played by the man with his face covered with his ancestors

The little saltimbanque turned like a wheel
With so much harmony
That the organ stopped playing
And the organist hid his face in his hands
With fingers like descendants of his destiny
Small foetuses which came out of his beard
New Indian cries
The angelic music of trees
The disappearance of the child

The saltimbanques lifted the great dumb-bells in their arms
And juggled with the weights

But each spectator looked in himself for the miraculous child
Century o century of clouds

Son visage m'échappe entièrement
C'est un homme sans tête

Un autre enfin avait l'air d'un voyou
D'un apache bon et crapule à la fois
Avec son pantalon bouffant et les accroche-chaussettes
N'aurait-il pas eu l'apparence d'un maquereau à sa toilette

La musique se tut et ce furent des pourparlers avec le public
Qui sou à sou jeta sur le tapis la somme de deux francs cinquante
Au lieu des trois francs que le vieux avait fixés comme prix des tours

Mais quand il fut clair que personne ne donnerait plus rien
On se décida à commencer la séance
De dessous l'orgue sortit un tout petit saltimbanque habillé de rose pulmonaire
Avec de la fourrure aux poignets et aux chevilles
Il poussait des cris brefs
Et saluait en écartant gentiment les avant-bras
Mains ouvertes

Une jambe en arrière prête à la génuflexion
Il salua ainsi aux quatre points cardinaux
Et quand il marcha sur une boule
Son corps mince devint une musique si délicate que nul parmi les spectateurs n'y
    fut insensible
Un petit esprit sans aucune humanité
Pensa chacun
Et cette musique des formes
Détruisit celle de l'orgue mécanique
Que moulait l'homme au visage couvert d'ancêtres

Le petit saltimbanque fit la roue
Avec tant d'harmonie
Que l'orgue cessa de jouer
Et que l'organiste se cacha le visage dans les mains
Aux doigts semblables aux descendants de son destin
Fœtus minuscules qui lui sortaient de la barbe
Nouveaux cris de Peau-Rouge
Musique angélique des arbres
Disparition de l'enfant

Les saltimbanques soulevèrent les gros haltères à bout de bras
Ils jonglèrent avec les poids

Mais chaque spectateur cherchait en soi l'enfant miraculeux
Siècle ô siècle des nuages

CŒUR COURONNE ET MIROIR

MON CŒUR PAREIL À UNE FLAMME RENVERSÉE

LES ROIS QUI MEURENT TOUR A TOUR

RENAISSENT AU CŒUR DES POÈTES

DANS CE MIROIR JE SUIS ENCLOS VIVANT ET VRAI COMME ON IMAGINE LES ANGES ET NON COMME SONT LES REFLETS

Guillaume

Apollinaire

The Cubist Painters

I: On painting

1.

The plastic virtues: purity, unity, and truth, keep nature in subjection.

The rainbow is bent, the seasons quiver, the crowds push on to death, science undoes and remakes what already exists, whole worlds disappear forever from our understanding, our mobile images repeat themselves, or revive their vagueness, and the colors, the odors, and the sounds to which we are sensitive astonish us, then disappear from nature — all to no purpose.

This monster beauty is not eternal.

We know that our breath has had no beginning and will never cease, but our first conceptions are of the creation and the end of the world.

However too many painters still adore plants, stones, the sea, or men.

We quickly get used to the bondage of the mysterious. And servitude ends by creating real delights.

Workers are allowed to control the universe, yet gardeners have even less respect for nature than have artists.

The time has come for us to be the masters. And good will is not enough to make victory certain.

On this side of eternity dance the mortal forms of love, whose accursed discipline is summed up by the name "nature."

Flame is the symbol of painting, and the three plastic virtues burn with radiance.

Flame has a purity which tolerates nothing alien, and cruelly transforms in its image whatever it touches.

Flame has a magical unity; if it is divided, each fork will be like the single flame.

Finally it has the sublime and incontestable truth of its own light.

.

Good western painters of this period hold to their purity, without regard to natural forces.

Purity is a forgetting after study. And for a single pure artist to die, it would be necessary for all pure artists of past ages to have never existed.

Painting purifies itself in Europe with the ideal logic which the older painters handed on to the new ones, as if giving them life.

And that is all.

This painter finds pleasure, that one, pain; one squanders his inheritance, another becomes rich, and still others have nothing but life.

And that is all.

You cannot carry around on your back the corpse of your father. You leave him with the other dead. You remember him, miss him, speak of him with admiration. And if you become a father yourself, you cannot expect one of your children to be willing to split in two for the sake of your corpse.

But in vain do our feet relinquish the soil which holds the dead.

To insist on purity is to baptize instinct, to humanize art, and to deify personality.

The root, the stem and the flower of the lily instance the development of purity to its symbolical blossoming.

.

All bodies stand equal before light, and their modifications are determined by this dazzling power, which molds them according to its will.

We do not know all the colors. Each of us invents new ones.

But above all, the painter must contemplate his own divinity, and the pictures which he offers to the admiration of men will confer upon them, likewise, the glory of exercising their divinity — if only for a moment. To achieve this, it is necessary to encompass in one glance the past, the present, and the future.

The canvas should present that essential unity which alone can elicit ecstasy.

Then nothing unstable will send us off half-cocked. We will not be suddenly turning back. Free spectators, we will not sacrifice our lives to our curiosity. The smugglers of appearances will not be able to get their contraband past the salt statues before our customs house of reason.

We will not go astray in the unknown future, which, severed from eternity, is but a word fated to tempt man.

We will not waste our strength on the too fugitive present; the fashionable, for the artist, can only be the mask of death.

The picture will exist ineluctably. The vision will be entire, complete, and its infinity, instead of indicating some imperfection, will simply express the relation between a newly created thing and a new creator, nothing more. Otherwise there would be no unity, and the connection which the different points of the canvas have with various dispositions, objects, and lights, would reveal only an assemblage of odds and ends, lacking all harmony.

For while an infinite number of creatures, each testifying to its creator, can exist without any one creation encroaching on the space of the others, yet it is impossible to conceive them all at once, and death results from their juxta-position, their union, their love.

Each god creates in his own image, and so do painters. Only photographers manufacture duplicates of nature.

.

Neither purity nor unity count without truth, which cannot be compared to reality, since it is always the same, subsisting beyond the scope of nature, which strives to imprison us in that fatal order of things limiting us to the merely animal.

Artists are above all men who want to become inhuman.

Painfully they search for traces of inhumanity, traces which are to be found nowhere in nature.

These traces are clues to truth, aside from which there is no reality we can know.

But reality will never be discovered once and for all. Truth is always new. Otherwise truth would be a system even more wretched than nature itself.

But such pitiful truth, more distant, less distinct, less real each day, would re-duce painting to a sort of plastic writing, intended simply to facilitate com-munication between people of the same race.

In our times, a machine to reproduce such signs would be quickly invented.

2.

Many new painters limit themselves to pictures which have no real subjects.

And the titles which we find in the catalogues are like proper names, which designate men without characterizing them.

There are men named Stout who are in fact quite thin, and others named White who are very dark; well now, I have seen pictures entitled *Solitude* containing many human figures.

In the cases in question, the artists even condescend at times to use vaguely explanatory words such as *Portrait, Landscape, Still-life;* however, many young painters use as a title only the very general term *Painting.*

These painters, while they still look at nature, no longer imitate it, and carefully avoid any representation of natural scenes which they may have observed, and then reconstructed from preliminary studies.

Real resemblance no longer has any importance, since everything is sacrificed by the artist to truth, to the necessities of a higher nature whose existence he assumes, but does not lay bare. The subject has little or no importance any more.

Generally speaking, modern art repudiates most of the techniques of pleasing devised by the great artists of the past.

While the goal of painting is today, as always, the pleasure of the eye, the art-lover is henceforth asked to expect delights other than those which looking at natural objects can easily provide.

.

Thus we are moving towards an entirely new art which will stand, with respect to painting as envisaged heretofore, as music stands to literature.

It will be pure painting, just as music is pure literature.

The music-lover experiences, in listening to a concert, a joy of a different order from the joy given by natural sounds, such as the murmur of the brook, the uproar of a torrent, the whistling of the wind in a forest, or the harmonies of human speech based on reason rather than on aesthetics.

In the same way the new painters will provide their admirers with artistic sensations by concentrating exclusively on the problem of creating harmony with unequal lights.

.

Everybody knows the story told by Pliny about Apelles and Protogenes. It clearly illustrates the aesthetic pleasure resulting solely from the contradictory harmonies referred to above.

Apelles landed, one day, on the Isle of Rhodes, and went to see the work of Protogenes, who lived there. Protogenes was not in the studio when Apelles arrived. An old woman was there, looking after a large canvas which the painter had prepared. Instead of leaving his name, Apelles drew on the canvas a line so subtle that nothing happier could be conceived.

Returning, Protogenes saw the line, recognized the hand of Apelles, and drew on the latter's line another line of another color, one even more subtle, so that it seemed as if there were three lines.

Apelles came back the next day, and again did not find his man; the subtlety of the line which he drew this time caused Protogenes to despair. The sketch aroused for many years the admiration of connoisseurs, who contemplated it with as much pleasure as if it had depicted gods and goddesses, instead of almost invisible lines.

·

The secret aim of the young painters of the extremist schools is to produce pure painting. Theirs is an entirely new plastic art. It is still in its beginnings, and is not yet as abstract as it would like to be. Most of the new painters depend a good deal on mathematics, without knowing it; but they have not yet abandoned nature, which they still question patiently, hoping to learn the right answers to the questions raised by life.

A man like Picasso studies an object as a surgeon dissects a cadaver.

This art of pure painting, if it succeeds in freeing itself from the art of the past, will not necessarily cause the latter to disappear; the development of music has not brought in its train the abandonment of the various genres of literature, nor has the acridity of tobacco replaced the savoriness of food.

3.

The new artists have been violently attacked for their preoccupation with geometry. Yet geometrical figures are the essence of drawing. Geometry, the science of space, its dimensions and relations, has always determined the norms and rules of painting.

Until now, the three dimensions of Euclid's geometry were sufficient to the restiveness felt by great artists yearning for the infinite.

The new painters do not propose, any more than did their predecessors, to be geometers. But it may be said that geometry is to the plastic arts what grammar is to the art of the writer. Today, scientists no longer limit themselves to the three dimensions of Euclid. The painters have been led quite naturally, one might say by intuition, to preoccupy themselves with the new possibilities of spatial measurement which, in the language of the modern studios, are designated by the term: the fourth dimension.[1]

·

Regarded from the plastic point of view, the fourth dimension appears to spring from the three known dimensions: it represents the immensity of space eternalizing itself in all directions at any given moment. It is space itself, the dimension of the infinite; the fourth dimension endows objects with plasticity. It gives the object its right proportions on the whole, whereas in Greek art, for instance, a somewhat mechanical rhythm constantly destroys the proportions.

Greek art had a purely human conception of beauty. It took man as the measure of perfection. But the art of the new painters takes the infinite universe as its ideal, and it is to this ideal that we owe a new norm of the perfect, one which permits the painter to proportion objects in accordance with the degree of plasticity he desires them to have.

Nietzsche divined the possibility of such an art:

"O divine Dionysius, why pull my ears?" Ariadne asks her philosophical lover in one of the celebrated dialogues on the Isle of Naxos. "I find something pleasant and delightful in your ears, Ariadne; why are they not even longer?"

Nietzsche, in relating this anecdote, puts in the mouth of Dionysius an implied condemnation of all Greek art.

Finally, I must point out that the fourth dimension — this utopian expression should be analyzed and explained, so that nothing more than historical interest may be attached to it — has come to stand for the aspirations and premonitions of the many young artists who contemplate Egyptian, negro, and oceanic sculptures, meditate on various scientific works, and live in the anticipation of a sublime art.

4.

Wishing to attain the proportions of the ideal, to be no longer limited to the human, the young painters offer us works which are more cerebral than sensual. They discard more and more the old art of optical illusion and local proportion, in order to express the grandeur of metaphysical forms. This is why contemporary art, even if it does not directly stem from specific religious beliefs, nonetheless possesses some of the characteristics of great, that is to say, religious art.

5.

It is the social function of great poets and artists to renew continually the appearance nature has for the eyes of men.

Without poets, without artists, men would soon weary of nature's monotony. The sublime idea men have of the universe would collapse with dizzying speed. The order which we find in nature, and which is only an effect of art, would at once vanish. Everything would break up in chaos. There would be no seasons, no civilization, no thought, no humanity; even life would give way, and the impotent void would reign everywhere.

Poets and artists plot the characteristics of their epoch, and the future docilely falls in with their desires.

The general form of an Egyptian mummy is in conformity with the figures drawn by Egyptian artists, and yet the ancient Egyptians were far from being all alike. They simply conformed to the art of their time.

To create the illusion of the typical is the social role and peculiar end of art. God knows how the pictures of Monet and Renoir were abused! Very well! But one has only to glance at some photographs of the period to see how closely people and things conformed to the pictures of them by these great painters.

Since of all the plastic products of an epoch, works of art have the most energy, this illusion seems to me quite natural. The energy of art imposes itself on men, and becomes for them the plastic standard of the period. Thus, those who mock the new painters are actually laughing at their own features, for people in the future will portray the men of today to be as they are represented in the most alive, which is to say, the newest art of our time. And do not tell me there are today various other schools of painting in whose images humanity will be able to recognize itself. All the art works of an epoch end by resembling the most energetic, the most expressive, and the most typical works of the period. Dolls belong to popular art; yet they always seem to be inspired by the great art of the same epoch. This is a truth which can easily be verified. Yet who would dare to say that the dolls which were sold at bargain counters, around 1880, were shaped by a sentiment akin to what Renoir felt when he painted his portraits? No one perceived the relationship then. But this only means that Renoir's art was sufficiently energetic to take hold of our senses, even though to the general public of the epoch in which he made his debut, his conceptions seemed absurd and foolish.

6.

There has been a certain amount of suspicion, notably in the case of the most recent painters, of some collective hoax or error.

But in all the history of art there is not a single instance of such general collaboration in artistic fraud or error. There are, indeed, isolated cases of mystification and blundering. But the conventional elements of which works of art are to a great extent composed guarantee the impossibility of such instances becoming general.

If the new school of painting were indeed an exception to this rule, it would be so extraordinary as to verge on the miraculous. As readily imagine all the children of some country born without heads, legs or arms, an obvious absurdity. There are no collective errors or hoaxes in art; there are only various epochs and dissimilar schools. Even if the aims pursued by these schools are not all equally elevated or equally pure, all are equally respectable, and, according to the ideas one has of beauty, each artistic school is successively admired, despised, and admired once more.

7.

The new school of painting is known as cubism, a name first applied to it in the fall of 1908 in a spirit of derision by Henri-Matisse, who had just seen a picture of some houses, whose cube-like appearance had greatly struck him.

The new aesthetics was first elaborated in the mind of André Derain,[2] but the most important and audacious works the movement at once produced were those of a great artist, Pablo Picasso, who must also be considered one of the founders: his inventions, corrobrated by the good sense of Georges Braque, who exhibited a cubist picture at the *Salon des Indépendants*[3] as early as 1908, were envisaged in the studies of Jean Metzinger, who exhibited the first cubist portrait (a portrait of myself) at the *Salon des Indépendants* in 1910, and who in the same year managed to induce the jury of the *Salon d'Automne*[4] to admit some cubist paintings. It was also in 1910 that pictures by Robert Delaunay, Marie Laurencin, and Le Fauconnier, who all belonged to the same school, were exhibited at the *Indépendants*.

The first group exhibition of the cubists, who were becoming more numerous, took place in 1911 at the *Indépendants;* room 41, which was devoted to their works, made a deep impression. There were the knowing and seductive works of Jean Metzinger; some landscapes, *Male Nude* and *Women with Phlox* by Albert Gleizes; *Portrait of Mme Fernande X* and *Young Girls* by Marie Laurencin; *The Tower,* by Robert Delaunay, *Abundance,* by Le Fauconnier, and *Landscape with Nudes,* by Fernand Léger.

That same year the cubists made their first appearance outside of France, in Brussels; and in the preface to the catalogue of this exhibition, I accepted on behalf of the exhibitors the appellations: cubism and cubist.

Towards the end of 1911 the exhibition of the cubists at the *Salon d'Automne* made a considerable stir, and Gleizes (*The Hunt, Portrait of Jacques Nayral*), Metzinger (*Woman with Spoon*), and Fernand Léger were ridiculed without mercy. A new painter, Marcel Duchamp, had joined the group, as had the sculptor-architect, Duchamp-Villon.

Other group exhibitions were held in November, 1911 (at the Galerie d'Art

Contemporain, rue Tronchet, Paris), and in 1912 (at the Salon des Indépendants; this show was marked by the debut of Juan Gris); in May of the same year another cubist exhibition was held in Spain (Barcelona welcomed the young Frenchmen with enthusiasm); finally in June, at Rouen an exhibition was organized by the Société des Artistes Normands (important for presenting Francis Picabia, who had just joined the new school). (Note written in September, 1912.)

.

Cubism differs from the old schools of painting in that it aims, not at an art of imitation, but at an art of conception, which tends to rise to the height of creation. There are four trends

In representing conceptualized reality or creative reality, the painter can give the effect of three dimensions. He can to a certain extent cube. But not by simply rendering reality as seen, unless he indulges in *trompe-l'oeil*,[5] in foreshortening, or in perspective, thus distorting the quality of the forms conceived or created.

I can discriminate four trends in cubism.[6] Of these, two are pure, and along parallel lines.

.

Scientific cubism is one of the pure tendencies. It is the art of painting new structures out of elements borrowed not from the reality of sight, but from the reality of insight. All men have a sense of this interior reality. A man does not have to be cultivated in order to conceive, for example, of a round form.

The geometrical aspect, which made such an impression on those who saw the first canvases of the scientific cubists, came from the fact that the essential reality was rendered with great purity, while visual accidents and anecdotes had been eliminated. The painters who follow this tendency are: Picasso, whose luminous art also belongs to the other pure tendency of cubism, Georges Braque, Albert Gleizes, Marie Laurencin, and Juan Gris.

.

Physical cubism is the art of painting new structures with elements borrowed, for the most part, from visual reality. This art, however, belongs in the cubist movement because of its constructive discipline. It has a great future as historical painting. Its social role is very clear, but it is not a pure art. It confuses what is properly the subject with images. The painter-physicist who created this trend is Le Fauconnier.

.

Orphic cubism is the other important trend of the new art school. It is the art of painting new structures out of elements which have not been borrowed from the visual sphere, but have been created entirely by the artist himself, and been endowed by him with fullness of reality| The works of the orphic artist must simultaneously give a pure aesthetic pleasure, a structure which is self-evident,[8] and a sublime meaning, that is, a subject. This is pure art. The light in Picasso's paintings is based on this conception, to which Robert Delaunay's inventions have contributed much, and towards which Fernand Léger, Francis Picabia, and Marcel Duchamp are also addressing themselves.

Instinctive cubism, the art of painting new structures of elements which are not borrowed from visual reality, but are suggested to the artist by instinct and intuition, has long tended towards orphism. The instinctive artist lacks lucidity and an aesthetic doctrine; instinctive cubism includes a large number of artists. Born of French impressionism, this movement has now spread all over Europe

Cézanne's last paintings and his water-colors belong to cubism, but Courbet[10] is the father of the new painters; and André Derain, whom I propose to discuss some other time, was the eldest of his beloved sons, for we find him at the beginning of the fauvist movement, which was a kind of introduction to cubism, and also at the beginnings of this great subjective movement; but it would be too difficult today to write discerningly of a man who so willfully stands apart from everyone and everything.

The modern school of painting seems to me the most audacious that has ever appeared. It has posed the question of what is beautiful in itself.

It wants to visualize beauty disengaged from whatever charm man has for man, and until now, no European artist has dared attempt this. The new artists demand an ideal beauty, which will be, not merely the proud expression of the species, but the expression of the universe, to the degree that it has been humanized by light.

The new art clothes its creations with a grandiose and monumental appearance which surpasses anything else conceived by the artists of our time. Ardent in its search for beauty, it is noble and energetic, and the reality it brings us is marvelously clear. I love the art of today because above all else I love the light, for man loves light more than anything; it was he who invented fire.

II: New painters

Picasso

If we were alert, all the gods would awaken. Born of the profound self-knowl-edge which humanity has kept of itself, the adored pantheisms resembling it have drowsed. But despite the eternal sleep, there are eyes reflecting humani-ties akin to these divine and joyous phantoms.

Such eyes are as attentive as the flowers whose desire it is always to behold the sun. O inventive joy, there are men who see with these eyes!

.

Picasso had been observing the human images which float in the azure of our memories, and partake of divinity, in order to damn the metaphysicians. How pious are his skies, alive with flights, and his heavy sombre lights, like those of grottoes!

There are children who have strayed off without having learned the cate-chism. They stop, and the rain stops falling. "Look, in those buildings there are people whose clothes are shabby." These children, whom one does not caress, know so much. "Mama, love me to death!" They can take things in their stride, and their successful dodges are mental evolutions.

The women one no longer loves come back to mind. By this time they have repeated their brittle ideas too often. They do not pray; they worship memories. Like an old church, they crouch in the twilight. These women renounce everything, and their fingers are itching to plait crowns of straw. At daybreak they disappear; they console themselves in silence. They cross many a threshold; mothers guard the cradles, so that the new-born may not inherit some taint; when they bend over the cradles, the little babes smile, sensing their goodness.

They often give thanks, and their forearms tremble like their eyelids.

Enveloped in frozen mist, old men wait unthinkingly, for it is only children who meditate. Inspired by far countries, animal struggles, locks of hardened hair, these old men beg without humility.

Other beggars have been used up by life. These are the infirm, the cripples, the bums. They are amazed to have come to the goal, which is still blue, but no longer the horizon. Old, they have become as foolish as kings who have too many troops of elephants bearing citadels. They are travellers who confound the flowers with the stars.

Grown old like oxen at twenty-five, the young have conducted nurselings to the moon.

On a clear day, certain women hold their peace; their bodies are angelic, and their glances tremble.

For a year, Picasso lived this type of damp painting, blue as the humid depth of an abyss, and full of pity.

Pity made Picasso harsher. The public squares held up one who had been hanged; he was stretched against the houses above the oblique passerby. The condemned awaited a savior. Miraculously the gallows hung athwart the roofs; the window panes flamed with flowers.

In rooms penniless painters drew fleecy nudes by lamplight. Women's shoes left by the bed were expressive of tender haste.

.

Calm followed this frenzy.

The harlequins go in splendid rags while the painting is gathering, warming or whitening its colors to express the strength and duration of the passions, while the lines delimited by the tights are bending, breaking off, darting out.

In a square room, paternity transfigures the harlequin, whose wife bathes with cold water and admires her figure, as frail and slim as her husband, the puppet.[11] Charming lilts mingle, and somewhere passing soldiers curse the day.

Love is good when one dresses it up, and the habit of spending one's time at home redoubles paternal feeling. The child brings the woman Picasso wanted glorious and immaculate closer to the father.

Primiparous mothers no longer expect the baby to arrive, because of certain ill-omened, raven-like chatterers.[12]

Christmas! They bring forth acrobats in the midst of pet monkeys, white horses, and dogs like bears.

The adolescent sisters, treading in perfect balance the heavy balls of the *saltimbanques,* impose on these spheres the radiant motion of worlds. These still adolescent youngsters have the anxieties of innocence; animals instruct them in the religious mystery. Some harlequins match the splendor of the women, whom they resemble, being neither male nor female.

The color has the flatness of frescoes; the lines are firm. But, placed at the frontiers of life, the animals are human, and the sexes are indistinct.

Hybrid beasts have the consciousness of Egyptian demigods; taciturn harlequins have their cheeks and foreheads paled by morbid sensuality.

These *saltimbanques* should not be confounded with actors. They should be observed with piety, for they celebrate mute rites with difficult dexterity. It is this which distinguishes Picasso from the Greek pottery painters whose designs he sometimes approaches. There, on the painted earthenware, bearded, garrulous priests offered in sacrifice animals, resigned and powerless. Here, virility is beardless, and shows itself in the sinews of thin arms; the flat part of the face and the animals are mysterious.

Picasso's taste for a running, changing, penetrating line has produced some probably unique examples of linear dry-point, in which he has not altered the general traits of things.

•

This *Malagueño*[13] bruised us like a brief frost. His meditations bared themselves silently. He came from far away, from the rich composition and the brutal decoration of the 17th century Spaniards.

And those who had known him before could recall swift insolences, which were already beyond the experimental stage.

His insistence on the pursuit of beauty has since changed everything in art.

•

Then he sharply questioned the universe. He accustomed himself to the immense light of depths. And sometimes he did not scorn to make use of actual objects, a two-penny song, a real postage stamp, a piece of oil-cloth furrowed by the fluting of a chair.[14] The painter would not try to add a single picturesque element to the truth of these objects.

Surprise laughs savagely in the purity of light, and it is perfectly legitimate to use numbers and printed letters as pictorial elements; new in art, they are already soaked with humanity.

It is impossible to envisage all the consequences and possibilities of an art so profound and so meticulous.

The object, real or illusory, is doubtless called upon to play a more and more important role. The object is the inner frame of the picture, and marks the limits of its profundity, just as the actual frame marks its external limits.

•

Representing planes to denote volumes, Picasso gives an enumeration so complete and so decisive of the various elements which make up the object, that these do not take the shape of the object, thanks to the effort of the spectator, who is forced to see all the elements simultaneously just because of the way they have been arranged.

Is this art profound rather than noble? It does not dispense with the observation of nature, and acts upon us as intimately as nature herself.

•

There is the poet to whom the muse dictates his chants, there is the artist whose hand is guided by an unknown being using him as an instrument. Such artists never feel fatigue, for they never labor, and can produce abundantly day in and day out, no matter what country they are in, no matter what the season: they are not men, but poetic or artistic machines. Their reason cannot impede them, they never struggle, and their works show no signs of strain. They are not divine and can do without their selves. They are like prolongations of nature, and their works do not pass through the intellect. They can move one without humanizing the harmonies they call forth. On the other hand, there are poets and artists who exert themselves constantly, who turn to nature, but have no direct contact with her; they must draw everything from within themselves, for no demon, no muse inspires them. They live in solitude, and express nothing but what they have babbled and stammered time and again, making effort after effort, attempt after attempt, just to formulate what they wish to express. Men created in the image of God, a time comes when they are able to rest to admire their work. But what fatigue, imperfections, crudenesses!

•

Picasso was the first type of artist. Never has there been so fantastic a spectacle as the metamorphosis he underwent in becoming an artist of the second type.

•

The resolve to die came to Picasso as he watched the crooked eyebrows of his best friend anxiously riding his eyes. Another of his friends brought him one day to the border of a mystical country whose inhabitants were at once so simple and so grotesque that one could easily remake them.

22

And then after all, since anatomy, for instance, no longer existed in art, he had to reinvent it, and carry out his own assassination with the practised and methodical hand of a great surgeon.

•

The great revolution of the arts, which he achieved almost unaided, was to make the world his new representation of it. Enormous conflagration.

•

A new man, the world is his new representation. He enumerates the elements, the details, with a brutality which is also able to be gracious. New-born, he orders the universe in accordance with his personal requirements, and so as to facilitate his relations with his fellows. The enumeration has epic grandeur, and, when ordered, will burst into drama. One may disagree about a system, an idea, a date, a resemblance, but I do not see how anyone could fail to accept the simple act of enumerating.

•

From the plastic point of view, it might be argued that we can do without so much truth, but, having once appeared, this truth became necessary. And then there are countries. A grotto in a forest where one cuts capers, a ride on a mule to the edge of a precipice, and the arrival in a village where everything smells of warm oil and spoiled wine. Or again, a walk to a cemetery, the purchase of a faïence crown (the crown of immortals), the mention of the *Mille Regrets,* which is inimitable. I have also heard of clay candelabra, which were so applied to a canvas that they seemed to protrude from it. Pendants of crystal, and that famous return from Le Havre.

As for me, I am not afraid of art, and I have not one prejudice with regard to the painter's materials.[15]

•

Mosaicists paint with marble or colored wood. There is mention of an Italian artist who painted with excrement; during the French revolution blood served somebody as paint. You may paint with whatever material you please, with pipes, postage stamps, postcards or playing cards, candelabra, pieces of oil cloth, collars, painted paper, newspapers.

For me it is enough to see the work; this has to be seen, for it is in terms of the quantity of an artist's production that one estimates the worth of a single work.

Delicate contrasts, parallel lines, a workman's craft, sometimes the object itself, sometimes an indication of it, sometimes an individualized enumeration, less sweetness than plainness. In modern art one does not choose, just as one accepts the fashion without discussion. Painting . . . an astonishing art whose light is illimitable.

Braque

Peaceful appearances in plastic generalization are joined once more in a temperate zone by the art of Georges Braque.

Georges Braque is the first of the new painters to have come in contact with the public after his aesthetic metamorphosis.

This important event took place in 1908, at the *Salon des Indépendants*.

.

Today the historic role of the *Salon des Indépendants* is becoming clear.[16]

The art of the 19th century — in which the integrity of the French genius again was manifested — was simply one long revolt against the academic, to which the rebels opposed authentic traditions, long ignored by the masters of the degenerate painting which bastions the citadel of the rue Bonaparte.[17]

Since its founding, the *Salon des Indépendants* has had a leading role in the evolution of modern art, and has successively revealed to us the trends and personalities which, for the last twenty-five years have made French painting today the only school which counts; it alone ransacks the universe for the logic of the great traditions, and it is always full of life.

It must be added that the *Salon des Indépendants* has shown no larger proportion of freakish works than have the official salons, for all their respectability.

Besides, the artistic culture of the present day is no longer based on a social discipline. And it is not the least merit of the work Braque showed in 1908, that it was in accord with the society in which the painter was evolving.

This feature, which had not appeared since the good period of Dutch painting, is the social element in the revolution of which Georges Braque was the spokesman.

It would have appeared two or three years earlier if Picasso had exhibited, but silence was necessary for him, and who knows — the abuse heaped on Georges Braque might have caused Picasso to turn aside from the difficult path he was the first to choose.

But in 1909, the revolution which had renewed the plastic arts was an accomplished fact. The pleasantries of the public and of the critics could not turn the tide.

Perhaps even more astonishing than the innovations introduced by Georges Braque's pictures, was the fact that one of the young painters had, without surrendering to the affectations of illustrators, restored to honor the order and craftsmanship without which there is no art.

•

Here, then, is Georges Braque. His role was heroic. His art calm and splendid. He is a serious craftsman. He expresses a beauty full of tenderness, and the pearly lusters of his pictures play on our senses like a rainbow. This painter is angelic.

He has taught the aesthetic use of forms so hidden that only certain poets had intimations of them. These luminous signs flare around us, but only a handful of painters have grasped their plastic significance. The work, particularly in its plainest realizations, contains a multiplicity of aesthetic elements which, no matter how new, are always in accord with the sentiment of the sublime, that which enables man to put order in chaos: what looks new must not be scorned, nor what is dirty, nor what we use, not even the imitation wood or marble of house painters. These appearances seem trivial, but when action requires, a man must begin with them.

I detest artists who are not of their time, and, just as the language of the people was for Malherbe[18] the proper language of his period, the means of the artisan, of the house painter, should be the most vigorous material expression of painting to the artist.

•

Georges Braque should be called "the verifier." He has verified all the innovations of modern art, and will verify still others.

Metzinger

Not one of the other young contemporary painters has known as much injustice or displayed as great resolution as the exquisite artist Jean Metzinger, one of the purest artists of our time. He has never failed to learn from events. During his painful journey in search of a method, Jean Metzinger stopped for a while in every one of the well-policed towns through which he passed.

We first encountered him in the elegant and modern city of neo-impressionism, whose founder and architect was Georges Seurat.

•

The true value of that great painter is still not understood.

In drawing, in composition, in the judiciousness of their contrasted lights, his works have a style which sets them apart from, and perhaps even above most of the works of his contemporaries.

25

No painter reminds me of Molière as does Seurat, of the Molière of the *Bourgeois Gentilhomme,* which is a ballet full of grace, lyricism, and common sense. And canvases like *The Circus* and *Le Chahut* are also ballets full of grace, lyricism, and good sense.

The neo-impressionist painters are those who, to quote Paul Signac, "have since 1882 initiated the technique known as divisionism, employing as a means of expression the optical mixture of tints and tones." This technique may be compared to the art of the Byzantine mosaicists; and I recollect that one day, in a letter to Charles Morice, Signac also referred to the Library at Siena.

This luminous technique, which imposed order on the discoveries of the impressionists, was first divined, and even applied by Delacroix, to whom it had been revealed while studying the pictures of Constable.

Seurat himself exhibited in 1886 the first divisionist painting — *A Sunday Afternoon on the Island of La Grande-Jatte.* It was he who carried furthest the contrast of complementary colors in the construction of pictures. His influence is felt today even at the *Ecole des Beaux-Arts,* and will be a seminal force in painting for some time to come.

.

Jean Metzinger played a role among the sophisticated and industrious divisionists. But the fact is that the colored minutiae of the neo-impressionists were used merely to indicate what elements formed the style of a period which, in nearly all its expressions, both industrial and artistic, seemed to the men of that period to be quite devoid of style. Seurat has drawn, with a precision that amounts to genius, certain pictures of the life of the period; in these works the firmness of style is rivalled by the almost scientific clarity of conception. (*Le Chahut* and *The Circus* almost belong to scientific cubism.) He reorganized the whole art of his time, in order to be able to freeze the characteristic postures of that fin de siècle, that wind-up of the 19th century, in which everything was angular, enervated, childishly insolent, sentimentally comical.

So beautiful an intellectual vision could hardly prolong itself, and once the picturesque style implied by 19th century art had been indicated, neo-impressionism ceased to play an interesting role. It brought no innovation, besides the contrast of complementary colors; it did, however, make clear the aesthetic value of what preceding schools had discovered since the end of the 18th century. Too many new possibilities began to stimulate the young painters. They could not freeze themselves in a technique which, being the last and strictest expression of an artistic period, had given its full measure with the first stroke [Seurat].

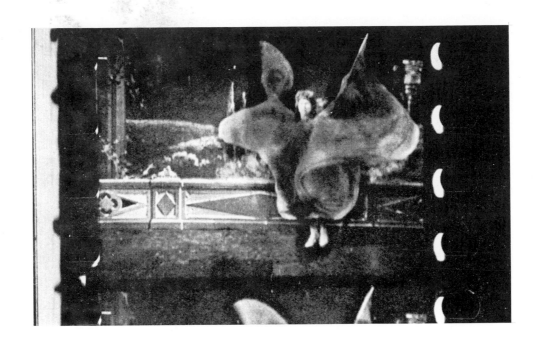

KOSTROWICKI dit

ALCOOLS

GUILLAUME APOLLINAIRE

[C'était toujours] Le principe de Chaque
vraie culture artistique de se laisser
diriger pas les ~~lois~~ éternelles hormes qui
obligeaient comme chaque tout organisme
sociale, de [tuseul] doit à obéir à certaine
~~nouves~~ lois

le caractère de la beauté moderne
changeait selon les tendances
se succédant et la logique des cette
tradition n'était soutenue que par des
personnalités vraiment créatrices par
des individualités dominantes contestés
en général par la critique et le public
absurde. ~~mais~~ Et cette tradition était
comme notre civilisation qui marchait
pas à pas des races humaines

de la main de Guillaume Apollinaire.

J. Apollinaire

Meilleurs souhaits pour 1915 !

24 - 12 - 14

Mon cher confrère,

votre adresse postale qui me
parvient à Nîmes, me donne
l'occasion de vous demander
de vos nouvelles, de vous
remercier de la journée charmante
passée chez vous à Fontainebleau
avant la guerre, de vous prier
de m'excuser auprès de la
maîtresse de maison si
je ne me suis pas excusé
à temps, de mettre à ses
pieds mes hommages très
respectueux et de vouloir
bien me croire votre admirateur
dévoué

Guillaume Apollinaire

Adresse : Guillaume Kostrowitzky
2e canonnier conducteur
38e reg. d'art. de camp.
70e batterie
Nîmes

31

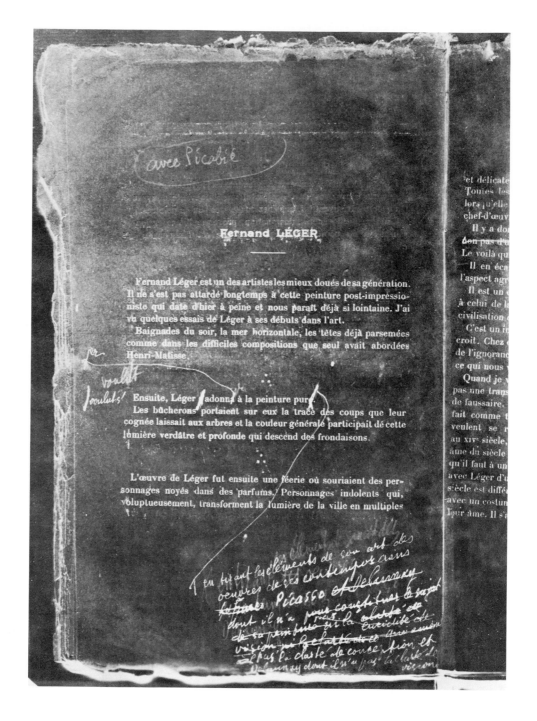

33

34

The technique became a tedious rule. The loud and colorful cries of the fauves were going off in the distance.[19] Jean Metzinger was drawn to them; and began to understand the symbolic significance of their colors and forms, for when that barbarous, but not savage city, given over to luxury and violent orgies, was deserted by the Barbarians, when the fauves had ceased to roar, nobody remained except peaceful bureaucrats who, feature for feature, resembled the officials of the rue Bonaparte, in Paris. And the kingdom of the fauves, whose civilization had seemed so powerful, so new, so astounding, suddenly took the aspect of a deserted village.

.

It was then that Jean Metzinger, joining Picasso and Braque, founded the cubist city. There disipline is rigorous, but is in no danger of becoming a system; more freedom is enjoyed there than anywhere else.

From his experience with the neo-impressionists, Jean Metzinger acquired a taste for minutiae, a taste by no means mediocre.

There is nothing unrealized in his work, nothing which is not the fruit of a rigorous logic, and if he ever fell into error (which I do not know or care to know), I am sure it was not by chance. His work will have the most authoritative documentary value for whoever will be interested in explaining our epoch. Thanks to Metzinger, we can distinguish between what has and what lacks aesthetic value in our art. A painting of Metzinger always contains its own explanation. This is perhaps a noble weakness, but it is certainly the result of great highmindedness, and is something unique, it seems to me, in the history of art.

The instant you catch sight of a painting by Metzinger, you feel the firm intent of the artist to be serious only about what is serious; and you feel that the occasion, in accordance with a method which I find excellent, furnishes him with the plastic elements of his art. But while he rejects nothing, he does not use anything haphazardly. His work is sound, more so, doubtless, than the work of most of his contemporaries. He will delight those who want to know the reasons for things; his reasons are such as to satisfy the mind.

.

The works of Jean Metzinger have purity. His meditations take beautiful forms whose harmony tends to approach sublimity. The new structures he is composing are stripped of everything that was known before him.

His art, always more and more abstract, but always charming, raises and attempts to solve the most difficult and unforeseen problems of aesthetics.

Each of his paintings contains a judgment of the universe, and his work is like the sky at night, when, cleared of clouds, it trembles with lovely lights.

35

There is nothing unrealized in his works; poetry ennobles their slightest details.

Gleizes

The powerful harmonies of Albert Gleizes should not be confused with the theoretical cubism of the scientific painters. I remember his first experiments. In these his desire to simplify the elements of his art could already be felt. At his debut, Albert Gleizes was confronted by movements which had succeeded; the last of the impressionists, the symbolists, some of whom had become intimists, the neo-impressionists, divisionists, fauves; his situation was not unlike that of the *Douanier* Rousseau, confronting the intellectualism and academicism of the official salons.

Then Gleizes came to understand the works of Cézanne, who had influenced the first cubists.

He developed the harmonies which must be rated with the most serious and significant plastic art of the last ten years.

His portraits are ample proof that with him, as with most of the new painters, the individualization of the object is not left to the spectator.

The pictures of Albert Gleizes, and those of many of the young artists, are often regarded as bashful generalizations.

And yet, in most of the new pictures the individual characters are delineated with decisiveness, and even, at times, an abundance of details; it is hard to see how this could escape anyone who watched the new painters working, or even looked at their canvases with some degree of attentiveness.

Weak generalization is rather the characteristic of intellectual painters of decadent periods. What individual characters appear in the paintings of a Henry de Groux, who generalizes the decadent sentiments of the imitators of Baudelaire, or in the pictures of a Zuloaga, who generalizes the conventional Spain of the last romantics? True generalization permits a more profound type of individualization, determined by light, as in the pictures of the impressionists—as with Claude Monet, Seurat, and even Picasso himself, artists who generalize sincerely, and refuse to specify the superficial traits of things. There is not a tree, a house, or a person whose individual characteristics the impressionists have kept.

It was an important painter who remarked, as he set to work on a portrait, that it would not be a good likeness.

But there is a type of generalization at once vaster and more precise. Thus the portrait plays a most important role with the new painters. They can always guarantee the likeness, and I have never seen one of their portraits which did not resemble the person painted.

.

What regard for reality, for individual traits, could painters like Bouguereau or Henner have had?[20]

With many of the new painters each plastic conception is individualized further by generalization, and this with a patience that is really extraordinary.

Because they are unconcerned with chronology, history, or geography, because they bring together elements heretofore kept separated, because a Gleizes attempts to dramatize objects, while concentrating on the artistic motions they elicit from him, it may be said that the goal of these new painters is a sublime precision.

.

All the figures in the pictures of Albert Gleizes are not the same figure, all trees are not the tree, all rivers, river; but the spectator, if he aspires to generality, can readily generalize figure, tree or river, because the work of the painter has raised these objects to a superior degree of plasticity in which all the elements making up individual characters are represented with the same dramatic majesty.

.

Majesty, this above all characterizes the art of Albert Gleizes. Thus he brings to contemporary art a startling innovation. Something which, before him, was found in but few of the modern painters.

This majesty arouses and provokes the imagination; considered from the plastic point of view, it is the immensity of things.

This is a powerful art. The pictures of Albert Gleizes were realized with a force comparable to that we feel in the pyramids, cathedrals, metal constructions, bridges, tunnels.

These works sometimes reveal awkwardness like those found in the great works humanity rates highest, because he who made them really aimed at the best possible work. The purest aim an artist can have in his work is to do his best; he is base indeed who is content to succeed without effort, without work, without giving all he has.

Laurencin

Our epoch has encouraged talented women to express themselves in art and literature.

37

Women bring to art a new vision, full of the joy of life.

There have been women painters in every age; the marvelous art of painting affords to the mind and imagination such subtle delights, it is really surprising that there have not been even more women painters.

16th century Italy produced Sophonisba Angussola, whose praises were sung by Lanzi and Vasari. Paul IV and the King of Spain vied for her works. Today these works are to be found in Madrid, Florence, Genoa and London. There are none in the Louvre. Born in Cremona around 1530, she soon excelled her master, Bernadino, and carried further the art of portrait painting. The moderns have sometimes confused her portraits with those of no one less than Titian himself. After having had the greatest success at the court of Philip II, she retired to Genoa, where she lost her sight. Lanzi says that she was regarded as the ablest art theorist of her century, and van Dyck, who came to hear her views, declared that he learned more from this blind old woman than from painters with the keenest sight.

Up till the present time, no other woman has achieved such glory through the plastic arts as Sophonisba Angussola.

·

Marie Laurencin[21] has contrived to express, in the major medium of painting, an entirely feminine aesthetic.

From her very first paintings, drawings and etchings, although these efforts were characterized only by a certain natural simplicity, it could be seen that the artist soon to be revealed would one day give expression to the grace and charm of the world.

Then she painted pictures in which the arabesques became delicate figures.

Ever since, in all her studies, this feminine arabesque, the feeling for which she has never lost, has appeared.

While a Picasso is concerned to exalt the thus far unrecognized picturesqueness of an object, so as to make it render its full quota of aesthetic emotion, Marie Laurencin, whose art is based on the work of Henri-Matisse and Picasso, devotes herself most of all to expressing the pictorial novelty of figures and objects. Her technique is less severe than that of Picasso, with whose work, nevertheless, her own is not without points of contact. These appear in the same enumeration of the elements which compose the picture. Thus she is faithful to nature, studying it relentlessly, but carefully rejecting whatever is without youth or grace, and she accepts the unknown elements of things only when they have a youthful aspect.

I believe she has been quite deliberate in orientating her art to the young and new, whether grave or gay. Feminine aesthetics, which, up to the present, have appeared almost exclusively in the applied arts, such as lacework and embroidery, could not but express first of all in painting the freshness of the feminine nature itself. Later on, other women will come, and express other feminine aspects of the universe.

As an artist, Laurencin may be placed somewhere between Picasso and the *Douanier* Rousseau. I mean this not in the sense of rank, but simply in the sense of kinship. Her art dances, like Salome, between that of Picasso, who, like a new John the Baptist, cleanses the arts with baptismal light, and that of Rousseau the sentimental Herod, the splendid, childlike old man, whom love brought to the outskirts of intellectualism, where the angels came to distract his grief, and prevent him from entering the frightful kingdom of which he had become the *Douanier;* finally, they admitted the old man to their company, and fitted him with heavy wings.

.

The young artists have already made clear in what honor they hold the works of this poor old angel that was Henri Rousseau the *Douanier,* who died towards the end of the summer of 1910. He might also be called the *Inhabitant of Delight,* considering both the neighborhood he lived in, and the qualities which make his paintings so charming to look at.

.

Few artists have been mocked during their lives as was the *Douanier,* and few men have faced with equal calm the hail of dirty digs and insults. This courteous old man always preserved his calm and good humor, and happily was able to find, in insults and mockeries, evidence that even the ill-intentioned could not disregard his work. This serenity, of course, was only pride. The *Douanier* was conscious of his power. He permitted himself to remark, once or twice, that he was the ablest painter of his time. And on more than one count this estimate is not so incorrect. He did indeed suffer from not having been educated in art when a youth (you feel this), but later, when he wanted to paint, he studied the masters passionately, and he is almost the only modern to have divined their innermost secrets.

.

His sole defects derive from an occasional excess of sentiment, for he could not always rise above his broad good humor, and this was in sharp contrast to his artistic venturesomeness, and the attitude he took in contemporary art.

But what positive qualities he had! It is most significant that the young artists were sensitive to just these qualities. He is to be congratulated above all in that he aimed at realizing, and not merely paying homage to, these qualities.

39

The *Douanier* went to the very end in his work, something very rare today. His paintings were made without method, system, or mannerisms. From this comes the variety of his work. He did not distrust his imagination any more than he did his hand. From this comes the grace and richness of his decorative compositions. He had taken part in the Mexican campaign, and his poetic and plastic recollections of tropical vegetation and fauna were most precise.

The result has been that this Breton, this old man who lived mostly in the suburbs of Paris, is without doubt the most extraordinary, the boldest, the most charming painter of the exotic. His *Snake Charmer* is evidence enough of this. But Rousseau was more than a decorator; he was not just an image-maker; he was a painter. It is this which makes comprehension of his work so difficult for some people. He had a feeling for order, as is shown, not only in his pictures, but also in his drawings, which are as ordered as Persian miniatures. His art had purity, as is shown in his feminine figures, in the structure of his trees, and in the harmonious song of the different tones of a single color, a style which is found only in French painting, and marks pictures as belonging to the French school, no matter who the artist. I refer, of course, to paintings of masters.

This painter had the most powerful will. How doubt this, having seen his careful detail, certainly not due to weakness, how doubt this, when before you the song of the blues and the melody of the whites are intermingling in his *Noce,* in which the face of an old peasant reminds one of certain Dutch men?

As a painter of portraits Rousseau is incomparable. A half-length portrait of a woman, in black and delicate greys, is carried even farther than a portrait by Cézanne. Twice I had the honor to sit for Rousseau in his small, light studio on the rue Perrel; I often watched him at work, and I know the care he gave to the tiniest details; he had the capacity to keep the original and definitive conception of his picture always before him until he had realized it; and he left nothing, above all, nothing essential, to chance.

Of all Rousseau's beautiful sketches, there is none so astonishing as the little canvas entitled *The Carmagnole.* It is the sketch for the *Centenaire de l'Indépendance,*[22] under which Rousseau wrote: *Auprès de ma blonde qu'il fait bon, fait bon, fait bon.*[23] . . .

Its nervous draughtsmanship, variety, charm, and delicacy of tones make this work's excellence. His pictures of flowers show the resources of charm and emphasis in the soul and hand of the old *Douanier.*

Let me remark in passing that all three painters (whom I have made no attempt to rank in order of value, limiting myself to the formulation of the points of contact between them), are all first rate portrait painters.

In the masterful work of Picasso, portraits hold an important place, and some of them (the *Portrait of Vollard* and the *Portrait of Kahnweiler*) will be ranked with masterpieces. The portraits of the *Douanier* Rousseau seem prodigious; it is still not possible to gauge their full beauty. Portraits are an important part of Marie Laurencin's work, too.

The prophetic element in the work of a Picasso, and the intellectual element which enters, in spite of everything, into the work of Rousseau, the work of an old man — these elements reappear in Laurencin, but transformed into a wholly new pictorial element. Like the dance, it is an infinitely gracious and rhythmical art of enumeration.

Here we find, transfigured and purified, everything which, until now, made for the originality and delicacy of feminine art in lace, embroidery, and Bayeux tapestry. Feminine art has acquired a major status, and will no longer be confounded with masculine. Feminine art is courtesy, joy, bravura. It dances in light and languishes in memory. It has never been imitative or been enslaved by perspective. It is a happy art.

Mario Meunier, then secretary to Rodin, and a fine translator of Sappho, Plato and Sophocles, told an amusing story about *The Toilet,* one of Laurencin's tenderest canvases. He was showing the sculptor some photographs of paintings by members of the fauves, and it so happened that among them was a reproduction of Laurencin's painting. "At any rate," said the illustrious old man, "here is one who is satisfied to be a *fauvette,* she knows what grace is, she is serpentine."

Exactly: feminine painting is serpentine, and perhaps that great artist in color and movement, Loie Fuller,[24] was the real forerunner of the feminine art of today, for she invented the successive lights in which painting, dance, and grace were combined into what is justly called: the serpentine dance.

In describing the work of another woman, the penetrating wit of Rodin lighted on the word serpentine.

Feminine art, the art of Laurencin, tends to become a pure arabesque, humanized by an attentive observation of nature; being responsive, it moves away from simple decoration, without loss of charm.

Gris

Here is the man who has meditated on everything modern, here is the painter who wants to conceive only new structures, whose aim is to draw or paint nothing but materially pure forms.

•

His antics were of a sentimental sort. He wept romantically, instead of laughing as in drinking songs. He still ignores the fact that color is a form of the real. He is a man intent on discovering the most minute elements of thought. One by one he has found them, and his first canvases have the appearance of preparations for masterpieces. Bit by bit, the little genii of painting assemble. The light hills are thronged. There is the bluish flame of gas-stoves, skies with forms like weeping willows, and damp leaves. He gives his pictures the wet quality of newly painted façades. Wall paper, a top hat, the disorder of advertisements on a high wall, — all these may very well serve to inspire a canvas by setting a limit to the painter's aims. Great forms thus acquire feeling. They are no longer tiresome. This art of ornamentation piously cherishes, and desperately tries to reanimate the last vestiges of classical art, such as the drawings of Ingres, and the portraits of David. Gris attains style, as Seurat did, but without the latter's originality as a theoretician.

Juan Gris has certainly taken this direction. His painting avoids the musical; that is, it seems to aim, above all, at scientific reality. Juan Gris has worked out in studies which relate him to Picasso, his only master, a type of drawing which at first seemed geometrical, but which was so individualized that it attained to style.

This art, if it perseveres in the direction it has taken, may end, not with scientific abstraction, but with that aesthetic arrangement which, after all, is the highest goal of scientific art. More forms may be suggested by the painter's ability, more colors, too, which are hints of forms. One could utilize objects whose capricious arrangement has undeniable aesthetic meaning. However, the impossibility of putting on canvas a man of flesh and blood, a mirror-wardrobe, or the Eiffel tower, will force the painter to return [from *collage*] to the authentic method of painting, or to limit his talents to the minor art of shop-windows — today many window displays are admirably arranged — or even to that of the upholsterer, or the landscape gardener.

The latter two minor arts are not without influence on the painter; the shop window should have a similar influence. It could hardly be harmful to painting, since it could not replace it in the representation of perishable objects. Juan Gris is too much a painter to renounce painting.

Perhaps we shall see him attempt the great art of surprise; his intellectualism, and the attentive study of nature should supply him with unexpected elements from which a style might issue even as a style issues today from the metal constructions of engineers: the style of the department stores, garages, railroads, airplanes. Since art today has a very limited social role, it is only fitting that it should occupy itself with the disinterested and scientific study — even without aesthetic aims — of its immense domain.

As influenced by Picasso's scientific cubism, the art of Juan Gris is too rigorous and too impoverished; it is a profoundly intellectual art, according to color a merely symbolic significance. Picasso's paintings are conceived in light (impressionism). Juan Gris is content with purity, scientifically conceived.

The conceptions of Juan Gris are always pure, and from this purity parallels are sure to come.

Léger

Léger is one of the gifted artists of his generation. He did not tarry long with post-impressionist painting — which was with us only yesterday, and already seems so remote. I have seen some of Léger's earliest experiments.

Night bathers, a horizontal sea, heads scattered, — as in the complicated compositions which, until then, Henri-Matisse alone had attempted.

After having made some completely new drawings, Léger wanted to devote himself to pure painting.

Lumberjacks bore on their persons traces of the blows their axes had left on the trees, and the general color partook of the greenish, deep light which falls across foliage.

.

After that Léger's work was a fairyland, in which persons drowning in perfumes smiled. There are indolent personages who voluptuously transform the light of the city into a multiplicity of delicate and shadowy colors, the memories of Norman shepherds. All the colors boil. Then steam forms, and when it is dissipated, the chosen colors remain; a kind of masterpiece was born of this ardor, *The Smoker*.

There is in Léger a desire to exact of a composition all the aesthetic emotion it can give. Right now he is lifting the landscape to the highest level of plasticity.

He discards whatever does not give his conception an agreeable and happy simplicity.

He was one of the first to resist the old instinct of the species "race," and to surrender happily to the instinct of civilization.

This instinct is resisted more widely than is supposed. This resistance, with some, became a grotesque frenzy, the frenzy of ignorance. With others, it consisted of turning to account whatever came to them through the five senses.

•

When I look at a picture by Léger, I am content. It is not a stupid transposition of the forger's craft. Nor is it a question of a work whose creator has done what everyone wants to do today. There are not a few who dream of refashioning souls or mediums of a kind found in the 14th or 15th centuries; there are others, still more skillful, who will make you a soul to fit the requirements of the Augustan age, or the time of Pericles, and all this in less time that it takes a child to learn to read. No, Léger is not one of those men who will believe that humanity changes from century to century, and thus confound God with a costumer, desirous to identify their costumes with their souls. Here is an artist comparable to those of the 14th or 15th centuries, to those of the time of Augustus and Pericles, neither more nor less; and in the attainment of glory and mastery, heaven helps the painter who helps himself.

•

Once, when he was up against it, the sculptor Manolo went to a picture dealer, who had a reputation for helping unrecognized talents.

Manolo proposed to sell the man some drawings, and had himself anounced.

The dealer sent back word that he did not know Manolo.

"Go tell him I am Phidias," replied Manolo.

But the dealer sent word that this name was unknown to him.

"Then tell him it was Praxiteles whom he refused to see." And the sculptor left.

But whoever was there, Phidias, Praxiteles, or Manolo, what is certain is that the soul of a Phidias cannot be reconstituted. Most men disguise themselves. That is why there are so few modern artists. The majority are disguised as such. The *salons* contain little but masks. I like authentic works of art. Those conceived by souls that were not made to order.

Welcome, beauties, tints, light colors, and you too, boiling forms! Pleasing threads of smoke are the emblem of civilization.

This crooked sky is the sky of our streets; it has been cut out and stood up. Here is the infinite sweetness of our raspberry roofs. What matter if this hand has six fingers, that man three feet?

Do not think this is mysticism. Not that I scorn the mystical. I am terrified in my admiration for it. Let him come, some day, the great mystical artist; let God summon him, compel him, give him orders. He will come; perhaps he is here now, quite close by; I know his name but cannot reveal it; one day it will be on everyone's lips; best not tell it: what happiness for him if he could disregard his mission, disregard his sufferings, and also that he is always in danger down here!

•

But Fernand Léger is not a mystic; he is a painter, a simple painter, and I rejoice as much in his simplicity as in the solidity of his judgment.

I love his art because it is not scornful, because it knows no servility, and because it does not reason. I love your *couleurs légères* [light colors], O Fernand Léger! Fantasy does not lift you to fairylands, but it grants you all your joys.

Here joy is expressed in the intention as well as in the execution. He will find other boiling points in form. The same orchards will bear even lighter colors. Other families will scatter themselves, like droplets from a water-fall, and the rainbow will come to dress in gorgeousness the tiny dancers of the ballet. The wedding guests hide one behind the other. Just another little effort to get rid of perspective, of that miserable tricky perspective, of that fourth dimension in reverse, of that infallible device for making all things shrink.

But this painting is liquid: the sea, blood, rivers, rain, a glass of water and our tears, wet kisses, the sweat of great efforts and deep fatigue.

Picabia

Coming from impressionism, like most of the contemporary painters, Francis Picabia, like the fauves, translated light into color. Thus he arrived at an entirely new art, for which color is no longer merely coloring, nor even a luminous transposition, for which color has no longer any symbolic significance, seeing that it is itself the form and light of whatever is represented.

Then he approached an art for which, as with Robert Delaunay, color is the ideal dimension. Consequently it has all the other dimensions. However, with Picabia the form is still symbolic, while the color is formal: a perfectly legitimate art, and surely a very subtle one. Color is saturated with energy, and its outmost points are prolonged in space. Here it is the medium which is the reality. Color no longer depends on the three known dimensions; it is color which creates them.

This art is as close to music as the opposite of music can be. One might say that the art of Picabia would like to stand, with respect to past painting, as music stands to literature, but one cannot say that it is musical itself. The truth is, music proceeds by suggestion; here, on the other hand, we are presented with colors which are not supposed to affect us as symbols, but as concrete forms. At the same time, without approaching new methods, an artist like Picabia here forgoes one of the principal elements of all painting: conception. In order for the artist to give the effect of having eliminated this element, color has to be formal (substance and dimension-proportion).

·

Let me add that the formulation of the title is, for Picabia, not separable, intellectually, from the work to which it refers. The title should play the part of an inner frame, as an actual object, or inscriptions exactly copied, do in the pictures of Picasso. It should ward off decadent intellectualism, and conjure away the danger artists always run of becoming literary. Analogous to Picabia's written titles, to the real objects, letters, and moulded ciphers in the paintings of Picasso and Braque, are the pictorial arabesques in the backgrounds of Laurencin's pictures. With Albert Gleizes this function is taken by the right angles which retain light, with Fernand Léger by bubbles, with Metzinger by vertical lines, parallel to the sides of the frame cut by infrequent echelons. The equivalent will be found, in some form or other, in the works of all the great painters. It gives pictorial intensity to a painting, and this is enough to justify its legitimacy.

It is by such methods that one guards against becoming literary; Picabia, for example, tried to give himself entirely to color, without ever daring, when approaching his subject, to grant it a personal existence. (I must remark here that a title does not mean the artist has approached a subject.)

Pictures like *Landscape, The Spring, Dance at the Spring,* are real paintings: colors form unities or contrasts, are oriented in space, and increase or decrease in intensity so as to elicit an aesthetic emotion.

·

It is not a question of abstraction, for these works give direct pleasure. Here surprise plays an important role. Can the taste of a peach be called abstract? Each picture of Picabia has a definite existence, the limits of which are set by the title. These pictures are so far from a priori abstractions that the painter can tell you the history of each one of them; *Dance at the Spring* is simply the expression of a plastic emotion experienced spontaneously near Naples.

Once purified, this art would have an immense range of aesthetic emotion. It could take as its motto the remark of Poussin: "Painting has no other end than the delectation and joy of the eyes."

Picabia, who seems to be looking for a dynamic art, might abandon the static picture for other means of expression (as Loie Fuller did). But I urge him, as a painter of pictures, to address himself to the subject (poetry), which is the essence of plastic art.

46

Duchamp

Marcel Duchamp's pictures are still too few in number, and differ too much from one another, for one to generalize their qualities, or judge the real talents of their creator. Like most of the new painters, Marcel Duchamp has abandoned the cult of appearances. (It seems it was Gauguin who first renounced what has been for so long the religion of painters.)

In the beginning Marcel Duchamp was influenced by Braque (the pictures exhibited at the *Salon d'Automne,* 1911, and at the *Gallery Rue Tronchet,* 1911), and by *The Tower* by Delaunay (*A Melancholy Young Man on a Train*).

•

To free his art from all perceptions which might become notions, Duchamp writes the title on the picture itself. Thus literature, which so few painters have been able to avoid, disappears from his art, but not poetry. He uses forms and colors, not to render appearances, but to penetrate the essential nature of forms and formal colors, which drive painters to such despair that they would like to dispense with them, and try to do so whenever possible.

To the concrete composition of his picture, Marcel Duchamp opposes an extremely intellectual title. He goes the limit, and is not afraid of being criticized as esoteric or unintelligible.

•

All men, all the beings that have passed near us, have left some imprints on our memory, and these imprints of lives have a reality, the details of which can be studied and copied. These traces all take on a character whose plastic traits can be indicated by a purely intellectual operation.

•

Traces of these beings appear in the pictures of Marcel Duchamp. Let me add — the fact is not without importance — that Duchamp is the only painter of the modern school who today (autumn, 1912) concerns himself with the nude: *King and Queen Surrounded by Swift Nudes; King and Queen Swept by Swift Nudes; Nude Descending a Staircase.*

This art which strives to aestheticize such musical perceptions of nature, forbids itself the caprices and unexpressive arabesque of music.

An art directed to wresting from nature, not intellectual generalizations, but collective forms and colors, the perception of which has not yet become knowledge, is certainly conceivable, and a painter like Marcel Duchamp is very likely to realize such an art.

47

It is possible that these unknown, profound, and abruptly grandiose aspects of nature do not have to be aestheticized in order to move us; this would explain the flame-shaped colors, the compositions in the form of an N, the rumbling tones, now tender, now firmly accented. These conceptions are not determined by an aesthetic, but by the energy of a few lines (forms or colors).

This technique can produce works of a strength so far undreamed of. It may even play a social role.

•

Just as Cimabue's pictures were paraded through the streets, our century has seen the airplane of Blériot, laden with the efforts humanity made for the past thousand years, escorted in glory to the [Academy of] Arts and Sciences. Perhaps it will be the task of an artist as detached from aesthetic preoccupations, and as intent on the energetic as Marcel Duchamp, to reconcile art and the people.

Appendix:

Duchamp-Villon

When sculpture departs from nature it becomes architecture. The study of nature is more necessary for sculptors than for painters, since it is easy to conceive of a painting free from nature. In fact, the new painters, while they study nature relentlessly, and even copy nature, refuse to accept the cult of natural appearances. It is actually only through conventions, amiably agreed to by the spectator, that it has been possible to correlate paintings with actual objects. The new painters have rejected such conventions, and some of them, opposing any return to the observation of these conventions, have chosen to introduce into their pictures, perfectly authentic elements, which, however, are alien to painting. For them, as for the writer, nature is a pure spring from which one may drink without fear of poisoning. Nature is their safeguard against the intellectualism of decadence, which is the greatest enemy of art.

Sculptors, on the other hand, can reproduce the appearances of nature (and not a few have done this). By the use of colors they can give us almost the illusion of livingness. However they can exact of nature even more than the immediate appearance of life, and can even imagine, enlarge or diminish, as did the Assyrian, Egyptian, negro, and south Pacific sculptors, forms endowed with great aesthetic life, so long as these forms are ultimately based on nature.

Attention to this basic limitation of sculpture justifies the work of Duchamp-Villon; when he wanted to escape this limitation, he turned directly to architecture.

A structure becomes architectural, and not sculptural, when its elements no longer have their justification in nature. Pure sculpture is subject to a singular necessity: it must have a practical purpose, whereas one can easily imagine an architectural work as disinterested as music, the art it most resembles. Think of the tower of Babel, the colossus of Rhodes, the statue of Memnon, the sphinx, the pyramids, the mausoleums, the labyrinths, the sculptured blocks of Mexico, the obelisks, menhirs, the triumphal or commemorative columns, *l'arc de triomphe,* the Eiffel tower, etc.

.

The whole world is covered with useless or almost useless monuments, which in any case are greater in their proportions than their purpose required. Indeed, the mausoleum, the pyramids are too large for tombs, and hence are quite useless; columns, even if, like the Trajan column or the Vendôme column, they are intended to commemorate events, are equally useless, since who is going to climb to the summits for the details of the historic scenes recorded there? What is more useless than a victory arch? The usefulness of the Eiffel tower postdated its disinterested construction.

However the feeling for architecture has been lost, so much so that the uselessness of monuments today is shocking, and appears to people as almost monstrous.

In revenge, while nobody will insist that sculptures be of use, without a practical end they become ridiculous.

Sculpture has for its practical end the representation of heroes, gods, sacred animals, images; and this artistic necessity has always been understood; it is responsible for the anthropomorphic character of the gods, for the human form finds its natural aesthetic most easily, and gives the greatest freedom to the fancy of the artist.

When sculpture abandons the portrait, it becomes nothing more than a decorative technique, destined to impart intensity to architecture (street lamps, allegorical statues for gardens, balustrades, etc.).

The utilitarian end aimed at by most contemporary architects is responsible for the great backwardness of architecture as compared with the other arts. The architect, the engineer should have sublime aims: to build the highest tower, to prepare for time and ivy the most beautiful of ruins, to throw across a harbor or river an arch more audacious than the rainbow, and finally to compose to a lasting harmony, the most powerful ever imagined by man.

49

Duchamp-Villon had this titanic conception of architecture. A sculptor and an architect, light is the only thing that counts for him; but in all the other arts, also, it is only light, incorruptible light, that counts.

Note:

Besides the artists of whom I have spoken in the preceding chapters, there are other living artists who in schools prior to cubism, in the contemporary schools or as independent personalities, are attached, whether willingly or not, to the cubist school.

Scientific cubism defended by Canudo, Jacques Nayral, André Salmon, Granié, Maurice Raynal, Marc Brésil, Alexandre Mercereau, Reverdy, Tudesq, André Warnod, and the author of this work numbers among its new supporters Georges Deniker, Jacques Villon and Louis Marcoussis.

Physical cubism supported in the press by the writers listed above, as well as by Roger Allard and Olivier Hourcade, can claim the talents of Marchand, Herbin and Véra.

Orphic cubism, defended by Max Goth and the author of his work, seems to be the pure tendency Dumont and Valensi propose to follow.

Instinctive cubism is an important movement; initiated some time ago, it is already a light outside of France. Louis Vauxcelles, René Blum, Adolphe Basler, Gustave Kahn, Marinetti, Michel Puy have supported certain individuals who base their work on this approach. The trend includes many artists including Henri-Matisse, Rouault, André Derain, Raoul Dufy, Chabaud, Jean Puy, van Dongen, Severini, Boccioni, etc.

In addition to Duchamp-Villon, the following sculptors have announced their adherence to the cubist school: Auguste Agéro, Archipenko and Brancusi.

Appendices to Reproductions:

(See Manuscript, page 29)
Best Wishes for 1915! 24-12-14

My dear Colleague,
Every genuine artistic culture has allowed itself to be guided by eternal norms, since every social organism must obey specific laws — The character of modern beauty has changed according to successive tendencies and the logic of this tradition has been only maintained by certain really creative personalities, by dominant individuals (who were) generally opposed by criticism and the absurdities of the public — And yet this tradition was like our whole civilization, which marched forward over the great Roman roads

(See Manuscript, page 31)
Your address which was forwarded to me at Nimes gives me the opportunity to ask about you, to thank you for the charming day I spent at your home in Fontainebleau before the war, to beg you to offer my apologies to the mistress of the house, if I did not do so at the time, to lay at her feet my respectful homage and to hope that you will believe that I am your devoted admirer, Guillaume Apollinaire.

Editor's Notes:

1. Apollinaire is obviously using the term "fourth dimension" metaphorically, in my opinion. But this position is denied by Paul M. Laporte in *"Cubism and Science"* in *"Journal of Aesthetics and Art Criticism,"* March 1949. My position was supported in a conversation several years ago with one of the most famous modern scholars who has a theory as to what Apollinaire meant and which I hope will one day be published in an article. I regret that the matter cannot be discussed here.
2. Derain's role in the evolution of cubism seems to have been limited to introducing Picasso and Braque (1909) to African sculpture, which was one of the sources of cubism. But cf. Kahnweiler's *"The Rise of Cubism"* in this series.
3. The first *Salon* (group exhibition of the work of living artists) took place in France in 1667 in the Palace of the Louvre, under the auspices of the French Royal Academy. Under Louis XV the *Salons* were held in the *grand salon carré,* hence the term *"Salon."* Only those affiliated with the Academy had the right to exhibit. The Revolution destroyed this privilege, opening the doors to everyone. The revolution of 1848 suppressed the jury of admission which had existed for more than a century, but the jury was restored after the political reaction in 1849. Since 1863 the *Salons* have been held annually. From about that time, however, the circumstance came about that, for the first time we know of in history, the best artists were ridiculed or ignored by organized society, and their works rejected by the official *Salon.* As a consequence, in December, 1884, Seurat, Redon, Signac, Valton, Guillaumin, Marie Bashkirtsheff, Bastien Lepage, and some other painters organized the first *Salon des Indépendants,* for unacademic artists. The precedent had been set for the *Salons des Indépendants* by the first (1874) Impressionist Exhibition, organized by Pissarro, Monet, Renoir, Cézanne, Sisley, Guillaumin, Berthe Morisot, Degas, Boudin, and twenty-one others (at the time only Manet among advanced artists was accepted by the official *Salon);* the impressionists held seven more Impressionist Exhibitions, the last in 1886. The majority of consequential artists since 1884 have shown in the *Salon des Indépendants* or its successor, the *Salon des Surindépendants.*
4. The first *Salon d'Automne* was held in Paris in 1903, and in it exhibited the fauves (not yet known by that name), Henri-Matisse, Rouault, Derain, Marquet, Vlaminck, etc., as well as J.-E. Blanche, Bonnard, and others: there was also a Gauguin Memorial Exhibition. It was at the Cézanne Memorial Exhibition at a subsequent *Salon d'Automne* that Picasso and Braque first saw works by that master.

5. *Trompe-l'oeil* (literally "deceive the eye") refers to extremely photographic or "realistic" representation in painting.

6. Apollinaire's four categories, which in truth are not very useful, have not passed into common usage.

7. The phrases here translated as "sight" and "insight" are in the original *réalité de vision* and *réalité de connaissance* (knowledge).

8. A propos of the phrase "a structure which is self-evident," it is interesting to note that A. N. Whitehead, in *"Modes of Thought"* (Cambridge, England, 1938), asserts that aesthetic experience itself can be regarded as a mode of the self-evident.

9. The vague category "instinctive cubism" serves Apollinaire as a device to include nearly every advanced painter of the time not participating in the cubist group itself: in his "Note" to the present work, he names among others, as "instinctive cubists," the fauves and the Italian futurists.

10. Courbet in fact had no discernible influence on the cubists; but cf. Kahnweiler, op. cit.

11. Apollinaire may have had in mind, in writing this passage the gouache now in the Lewisohn collection.

12. In this, and the following paragraphs of the section, Apollinaire is describing the content of Picasso's "saltimbanque" (mountebank) period (1905).

13. *"Malagueño,"* a native of Malaga, the province in Spain from which Picasso came.

14. Here Apollinaire is apparently referring to *papier collé* (literally "glued paper"), a medium invented by the cubists, in which papers of various kinds were glued to the picture for their value as "objects" rather than representations.

15. Apollinaire is defending the medium of *papier collé* and *collage* (the latter being the medium in which anything feasible can be glued to the canvas).

16. Cf. note 3 above; there is a detailed account of the various *Salons des Indépendants* in R. H. Wilenski's *"Modern French Painters"* (N. Y., 1939; 2nd ed., London, 1944).

17. "The citadel of the rue Bonaparte" is the *École des Beaux-arts,* which is situated on the street of that name, in Paris. There academic painting is taught to young painters, just as it is in the United States in various academies, leagues, institutes, museum schools, and universities.

18. François de Malherbe (1555–1628), French poet and critic, who was concerned with the standards of poetic technique in his epoch.

19. This paragraph plays on the literal meaning of *fauve* ("wild beast"); an account of the movement may be found in Wilenski, op. cit. It is hoped to publish Georges Duthuit's book on the subject in this series.

20. Bourgereau and Henner were successful French academic painters of the latter part of the 19th century.

21. Laurencin would hardly be considered, by a modern historian, as a cubist, no more than certain other painters mentioned in this book — e. g., Marcel Duchamp who, from one point of view is closer to the futurists, and from another, to the dadaists; or Picabia, or Duchamp-Villon.

22. The Centenary of Independence (of the first French Republic).

23. The words are from a popular French song.

24. Loie Fuller (1868–1928), American dancer, in early life an elocutionist and temperance lecturer. Later she toured with stock companies, and in 1891 appeared in New York as a dancer. She gained fame for her invention of the so-called serpentine dance, by which, with the manipulation of voluminous draperies and the artistic use of colored lights, she achieved new effects in dancing. She had a school of the dance in Paris; she wrote *"Fifteen Years of a Dancer's Life"* (N. Y., 1913). Mallarmé and other poets wrote about her. See the article by Clare de Morinni in *Chronicles of the American Dance,* edited by Paul Magriel (New York, 1948).

ET MOI AUSSI JE SUIS PEINTRE

Album d'idéogrammes lyriques et coloriés, par GUILLAUME APOLLINAIRE

Accompagnés d'un portrait de l'auteur

gravé sur bois, par PIERRE ROY, d'après GIORGIO DE CHIRICO

Tirage limité à 200 exemplaires numérotés

Prix : 10 Francs

Pour les Abonnés des *Soirées de Paris* : 7 fr. 50

Je soussigné, déclare souscrire à _____ *exemplaire* _____ *de* **Et moi aussi je suis peintre** *par Guillaume Apollinaire.*

Nom _____

Adresse _____

Date _____

Signature : _____

Renvoyer le présent bulletin, dûment rempli et signé, aux *Soirées de Paris*, 278, boulevard Raspail, et y joindre le montant de la souscription en mandat poste ou autrement.

Bibliographical Notes on Apollinaire and Cubism by Bernard Karpel

Part 1: *The Man*

"On dira que je ne suis pas avancé très loin dans l'exploration de cette âme. A cela je repondrai que si l'enchanteur m'avait dévoilé tous ses secrets, je l'eusse enfermé déjà dans un cercle magique et fait entrer au tombeau."

André Breton (1917)[39]

That the death of Apollinaire in 1918 should have given rise to expressions of grief, devotion and homage by the intellectuals of Paris is not surprising. Tristan Tzara and Francis Picabia broke into speech briefly in *Dada* (Dec. 1918). But soon a flood of commentary poured forth: special numbers of *S I C* (1919),[31] *Nouvelles Littéraires* (1923), *Vient de Parâitre* (1923), *Images de Paris* (1924),[32] and the most outstanding of these tributes *L'Esprit Nouveau* (1924).[33] Faithful disciples issued their testimonials: Roch Grey (1918),[43] Toussaint-Luca (1920),[52] André Salmon in *Nouvelle Revue Française* (1920),[49] and even in a novel of Montmartre *La Negresse du Sacré-Coeur* (1920),[50] André Billy in *Apollinaire vivant* (1923).[37] Truly they bore witness that, in the words he himself had used to introduce Baudelaire "en lui s'est incarné pour la première fois l'esprit moderne."[24]

What is surprising, however, is that this absorption in a poet of the new spirit — whom some contend to be the seminal influence on "the metaphysical and philosophical literature which launched cubism"[98] — has not diminished with the passage of two decades and another world conflict. This Abel translation was published as the first of a series on "The documents of modern art"[12] in 1944, and soon went out-of-print. On its heels Bonfante[14a] issued a partial French reprint addressed to Italian readers while Peri,[13] De Libero[13a] and Minoia[14] issued a complete Italian text. Six critical works, exclusive of periodical contributions, appeared in 1945 alone: Aegerter and Labracherie,[15] René Guy Cadou,[40] Louise Faure-Favrier,[42] Carola Giedion-Welcker,[8] André Rouveyre.[47] That these were not to be the end of a post-war exploration of its traditions is warranted by the re-publication of Apollinaire's magnificent manifesto "L'Esprit moderne et les poètes,"[27] the excellent anthology by Guillermo de Torre,[15] and the recent study by a member of his circle, André Billy.[38]

The literature *by* and *on* Apollinaire is too exhaustive, perhaps irrelevant as a totality, to record here. Besides, it has been documented in great detail by Elie Richard (1924),[1] Hector Talvart-Joseph Place (1928),[2] Ernst Wolf (1937),[6] Jeanin Moulin (1939),[7] and Henri Parisot (1947)[9] as well as in other sources noted in numbers 2, 3, 4, 5, 8. There is not, to our knowledge, a listing of *all* periodical contributions and lesser pieces by Apollinaire, although Wolf gives an invaluable record for the years 1901–1905. However, Richard suggests in his bibliography how vast this task must be, since he notes twenty-seven magazines and journals which represent "collaboration" by Apollinaire. Unfortunately, many of these serials are absent from or meagerly held by American libraries. The bibliographical problem is embarrassed, moreover, by the complexity of these references. Note a simple example: Apollinaire wrote "Connaissance de soi-même" on Henri Matisse in *La Phalange* (1907)[16] which was subsequently published in *Cahiers d'Art* (1931) and also incorporated, in English translation, in a full monograph on "Henri-Matisse," simultaneously issued in New York and Paris the same year.[17] The problem of tracing Apollinaire's articles on art and artists in such periodicals as *La Phalange*[15] and *Le Mercure de France*,[29] their eventual modifications and reappearances in his anthologies *Il y a*[28] and *Anecdotiques,*[29] or his contributions in *S I C*[31] or *Les Soirées de Paris*[15] and their metamorphoses into English and other languages[18] — this is too considerable to undertake here.

Since the essence of Apollinaire — from the point of view of the plastic arts — is incorporated in "Les Peintres cubistes," only the specialist would find an intensive investigation of value. But it is rewarding to know that the early article on modern painting published in *Der Sturm* (1913)[19] was recently issued in re-translation from the German (1939),[20] that the use of the term *surrealism*, so frequently ascribed to the June 24, 1917 performance of "Les Mamelles de Tirésias,"[26] was antedated in Apollinaire's statement on *"Parade* et l'esprit nouveau" (May 1917),[25] that even Billy's recent anthology (1947)[38] brings to light eight previously *unpublished* items, and that in libraries and private collections there must be little-known documents which wait the day of discovery and interpretation.[22, 23, 30] In his tragically short life, Apollinaire manifested an abundance of literary creation that matched his gargantuan conceptions of life itself.

Bibliographical References

1. RICHARD, ELIE. Bibliographie sommaire. *In* L'Esprit Nouveau. Apollinaire. p[86–87] Paris, Librairie Jean Budry [1924].[33] *Also published in Les Images de Paris.*[32] *Includes brief critical notes.*

2. TALVART, HECTOR *et* PLACE, JOSEPH. Bibliographie des auteurs modernes de langue française (1801–1941). vol. 1, p79–85 Paris, Chronique des Lettres Françaises, 1928. *Inclusive list of works, with a selection of books and articles on Apollinaire. Also issued as* La Fiche bibliographique française *Établié par Hector Talvart.* [*La Rochelle, Jean Foucher, 1924?*]. *Supplemented by Moulin.*[7]

3. TAUPIN, RENE. L'Interprétation américaine de la poésie française contemporaine. Paris, Les Presses modernes, 1929. *"Contenant une bibliographie des travaux américains consacrés à G. Apollinaire . . . Sur G. Ap., p23,139" (Moulin)*

4. FABUREAU, HUBERT. Guillaume Apollinaire. p91–94 Paris, Nouvelle Revue Critique, 1932 (Collection critique. Célébrités contemporaines. sér2, no9)

5. THIEME, HUGO PAUL. Bibliographie de la littérature française de 1800 à 1930. vol. 1, p38–39 Paris, E. Droz, 1933. *Contains a chronological list of works and articles by Apollinaire as well as reviews in books and periodicals.*

6. WOLF, ERNST. Guillaume Apollinaire und das Rheinland. p154–164 [Bonn?] Von Ernst Wolf aus Dortmund-Husen, 1937. *Doctoral dissertation. Includes lengthy bibliography with detailed history of periodical contributions by Apollinaire for 1901–1905. Includes occasional notes.*[18-19]

7. MOULIN, JEANIN. Manuel poétique d'Apollinaire, enrichi de textes rares et inédits. p117–123 Bruxelles, 1939 (Journal des poètes. Les cahiers. no62) *"Bibliographie Apollinarienne" supplements and brings up-to-date the comprehensive list by Talvart and Place.*[2]

8. GIEDION-WELCKER, CAROLA. Die neue Realität bei Guillaume Apollinaire. p43–49 Bern-Bümpliz, Benteli, 1945. *List of works by Apollinaire, p43–45; important works on Apollinaire, p46–49.*

9. PARISOT, HENRI. Bibliographie. *In* BILLY, ANDRE. Apollinaire. p227–235 Paris, Pierre Seghers, 1947 (Poètes d'aujourd'hui.8) *Includes observations not noted in previous compilations.*

BIBLIOGRAPHIES are also noted in no51,57 and elsewhere. Inevitably there is considerable duplication and occasionally unique references.

Selected Writings

10. APOLLINAIRE, GUILLAUME. [Méditations esthétiques] Les Peintres Cubistes. (Première série – Pablo Picasso – Georges Braque – Jean Metzinger – Albert Gleizes – Juan Gris – Mlle Marie Laurencin – Fernand Léger – Francis Picabia – Marcel Duchamp, etc.). Ouvrage accompagné de 46 portraits et reproductions hors texte. Neuvième édition. 84p plus plates Paris, Eugène Figuière et cie, éditeurs, 1913. (Tous les arts, collection publiée sous la direction de M. Guillaume Apollinaire) *"Méditations esthétiques," p5–27. "Peintres nouveaux," p31–84. "Appendice: Duchamp-Villon," p79–82. "Note," p83–84. The cover title emphasizes "Les Peintres Cubistes"; the running title is "Méditations esthétiques." Supplementary plates include 5 portraits. Ten copies issued on "Japon impérial." "Privilège copyright in the United-States by Guillaume Apollinaire, 20 mars 1913." Works by Picasso, Braque, Metzinger,† Gleizes,† Laurencin, Gris,† Léger, Picabia† and Duchamp† are reproduced († indicates portrait photograph) which were partly duplicated in Wittenborn[12] whose editor substituted new pictorial matter and paragraph captions. Kahnweiler mentions that "all the theoretical parts of each chapter were*

written . . . with the assistance of the painter." In "Der Sturm" for Dec. 1912, Apollinaire refers to his book Méditations Esthétiques (Figuière 1912). De Torre includes in his anthology an appendix dated (1912). Both Richard and Fabureau refer to a title "Les Peintres cubistes," dated 1912, although Talvart and many others refer only to an edition of 1913. Octave Béliard reviewed "Les Peintres cubistes" in Les Hommes du Jour, June 14 1913 and A. Soffici in La Voce no26 1913. Additional reviews are noted in nos74,81,110.

The Figuière text was also issued in 1922 by Editions Athena, apparently unauthorized. Only the French text of the first section was included in Bonfante,14a but a fuller text was published in translation by Tre Venezie,13 O.E.T.,13a Balcone,14 and Poseidon.15 The available English translations are by Abel12 and Knoblauch.

11. APOLLINAIRE, GUILLAUME. Aesthetic meditations. On painting, the cubist painters. The Little Review Spring, Winter, Autumn 1922.
"Translated by Mrs. Charles Knoblauch, for the Société Anonyme." Includes illustrations. First series, v8, no2, p7–19 Spring 1922. Second series, v9, no2, p49–60 Winter 1922, and v9, no3, p41–59 Autumn 1922.

12. APOLLINAIRE, GUILLAUME. The cubist painters, aesthetic meditations 1913. 35p illus. New York, Wittenborn, 1944. (The documents of modern art no. 1, edited by Robert Motherwell)
"Translated from the French by Lionel Abel." Preface by Robert Motherwell. Bibliography, p[6]. Revision issued 1949.

13. APOLLINAIRE, GUILLAUME. I pittori cubisti (con una letterà di Picasso sull'arte). [A cura di Giorgio Peri]. 88p plus 18 plates Padova, "Le Tre Venezie," 1945.
"Fuori testo: Picasso — Letterà sull' arte pag. I–VIII." Only 4 illustrations originally appeared in 1913 edition of Apollinaire to which the text corresponds. Introduction by Peri, p7–10.

13a. APOLLINAIRE, GUILLAUME. I pittori cubisti. Roma, Ed. O.E.T., 1945.
Translation and preface by Libero de Libero.

14. APOLLINAIRE, GUILLAUME. I pittori cubisti. 99p plus plates Milano, "Il Balcone," 1945 (Testie documenti d'arte moderna. 2)
Introduction by Carlo Carra. Translation by Franca Minoia.

14a. BONFANTE, EGIDIO e RAVENNA, JUTI. Artè cubista, con le Méditations esthétiques sur la peinture di Guillaume Apollinaire. 225p incl 67 plates (some colored) Venezia, Ateneo, 1945.
Reprints only first part of "Les Peintres cubistes" in French, p13–25. Bibliography, p27–28. Primarily a collection of classified plates with brief introductions, p31–221.

15. TORRE, GUILLERMO DE. Guillaume Apollinaire, estudio preliminar y páginas escogidas. 33 reproducciones 290p plus plates Buenos Aires, Poseidon, 1946. (Criticos e historiadores de arte)
Páginas escogidas (p89–285): Meditaciones estéticas: los pintores cubistas. — Otros pintores. — Poemes sobre pintores. — Un "marchand." — Un manifiesto.— Una anticipación del superrealismo. — Imágenes de escritores. — Fragmentos novelescos. Meditaciones estéticas, p91–161, includes an Apéndice: Notas sobre et simulteismo, p159–161, dated (1912) which does not appear in editions dated 1913 examined by the compiler. "Henri Matisse," p181–184, originally appeared in La Phalange.16 "El aduanero Henri Rousseau," p165–179, was first published in Les Soirées de Paris no20 1913, and subsequently in Il y a.28

16. APOLLINAIRE, GUILLAUME. Connaissance de soi-même. La Phalange Dec 15, 1907.
Later published in Cahiers d'Art. v6, no5–6, p316 1931. Also translated in de Torre.15

17. APOLLINAIRE, GUILLAUME. Knowing oneself. In Henri-Matisse. p96 Paris, Cahiers d'Art, New York, E. Weyhe, 1931.
The source is given as La Phalange Nov 15 1907.

18. APOLLINAIRE, GUILLAUME. Réalité, peinture pure. Der Sturm v3, no138–39, p224 Dec 1912.
"Der Text ist deutsch, trotz des französischen Titels, offenbar eine Uebersetzung aus dem Französischen, im wesentlichen

*eine rein referierende, wörtliche Wieder-
gabe von Bemerkungen des Malers Robert Delaunay über seine Aesthetik. Der
französische Text befindet sich heute in
Il Y A unter dem Titel "Notes," nicht in
"Les Peintres Cubistes." (Ernst Wolf[6])*

19. APOLLINAIRE, GUILLAUME. Die moderne
Malerei. Der Sturm v3, no148–149, p272
Feb 1913.
*"Ueber den Kubismus, seine Beziehungen
zur modernen französischen Dichtung
(Dramatismus) und zum deutschen Ex-
pressionismus in der Malerei. Wahr-
scheinlich von Apollinaire für den
"Sturm" eigens (französisch) geschrieben.
Die Definitionen der verschiedenen ku-
bistischen Richtungen aus "Les Peintres
Cubistes." Wolf incorrectly cites this title
as: Die Neue Malerei. Issued in French in
1939.[20]*

20. APOLLINAIRE, GUILLAUME. La Peinture
moderne. Paris. S.L.N.D., 1939.
*"Traduction du français par Jean Jacques,
retraduit de l'allemand par Anatole Dela-
grave."*

21. APOLLINAIRE, GUILLAUME. L'Antitradition
futuriste, manifeste — synthèse. Milan,
Direction du mouvement futuriste, 1913.

22. APOLLINAIRE, GUILLAUME. Et moi aussi je
suis peintre. Album d'idéogrammes lyriques et coloriés par Guillaume Apollinaire, accompagnés d'un portrait de
l'auteur gravé sur bois par Pierre Roy
d'après Georges de Chirico. [projected
only]
*"Ouvrage annoncé en 1914; n'a jamais
été publié, ni peut-être composé" (Fabureau[4]). Reproduced, p. 53.*

23. APOLLINAIRE, GUILLAUME. A propos de
l'art des noirs. *In* Sculptures nègres. 24
phototypies précédées d'un avertissement
de Guillaume Apollinaire et d'un exposé
de Paul Guillaume. [7]p plus 24 plates
Paris, Chez Paul Guillaume, 1917.
*Printed Apr 25 in edition of 63 de luxe
copies. Apparently not listed in bibliographies examined by the compiler. (Copy
in Metropolitan Museum Library, New
York)*

24. APOLLINAIRE, GUILLAUME. Introduction. *In*
Baudelaire, Charles Pierre. L'Oeuvre poétique de Charles Baudelaire. . . . Intro-

duction et notes par Guillaume Apollinaire. Paris, Bibliothèque des Curieux,
1917 (Les Maîtres de l'amour)

25. APOLLINAIRE, GUILLAUME. *Parade* and the
new spirit. Dance Index (New York) v5,
no11–12, p268–269 Nov–Dec 1946.
*Special number: "Picasso and the ballet"
by William S. Lieberman. "Apollinaire's
Parade et l'Esprit nouveau was originally
published in the Ballets Russes program
for the May 1917 season at the Théâtre
du Châtelet." The author points out that
in this introduction the term "sur-réa-
lisme" is employed, antedating its usual
reference to the June 24, 1917 performance of "Les Mamelles de Tirésias."[26]*

26. APOLLINAIRE, GUILLAUME. Les Mamelles
de Tirésias. Drame surréaliste en deux
actes et un prologue. Paris, Editions Sic,
1918.
*"The word surréalisme was first coined in
this text" (Pierre Berès surrealist catalog,
New York, 1948). This typical statement
is refuted by William S. Lieberman.[25] Albert-Birot in Rimes et Raisons[34] mentions that the term was added by Apollinaire just before submitting the text to
the printer. Another edition, with six unpublished portraits by Picasso, was issued
by Editions du Bélier, Paris, 1946.*

27. APOLLINAIRE, GUILLAUME. L'Esprit nouveau et les poètes. Le Mercure de France
p384–396 Dec 1 1918.
*Issued separately by Haumont, Paris,
1946.*

28. APOLLINAIRE, GUILLAUME. Il y a. Préface
de Ramon Gomez de la Serna. 245p Paris,
A. Messein, 1925 (Collection La Phalange)
*"Peintres," p127–206. Essays written from
1907–1918, poems from 1895–1918.*

29. APOLLINAIRE, GUILLAUME. Anecdotiques.
290p Paris, P. V. Stock, 1926.
*Based on material published in Le Mer-
cure de France, 1911–1918.*

30. APOLLINAIRE, GUILLAUME. [Fragment of a
mss. beginning: "Chaque vraie culture
artistique. . . .] n.d.
*Formerly in the collection of Paul Elu-
ard, now in the Museum of Modern Art
Library, New York. Reproduced here, p.
29.*

Special Numbers on Apollinaire

31. S I C. Nos37–39 Jan–Feb 15 1919.
"Numéro composé en memoire de Guillaume Apollinaire," v4, p281–308. In this "revue de P. Albert-Birot, qui bataillait opiniâtrement en faveur de l'art moderne, on y retrouvait Apollinaire, Reverdy, les tenants du cubisme littéraire et du futurisme" (Nadeau[45]). "Les tendances nouvelles, interview avec Guillaume Apollinaire" appears in no8–10, p[2–3] Aug–Oct 1916, although contributions by or on Apollinaire appeared in almost every issue.

32. IMAGES DE PARIS. Jan–Feb 1924, Sept 1924.
Première partie: Guillaume Apollinaire. — Deuxième partie: Les Inédits de Guillaume Apollinaire. Elie Richard's bibliography[1] was prepared for this occasion and subsequently appeared in L'Esprit Nouveau.

33. L'ESPRIT NOUVEAU. No26 July 1924.
"Numéro spécial consacré à Guillaume Apollinaire." Also issued as separate by Librairie Jean Budry with new cover by Picasso. [98]p Includes portraits and drawings, facsimiles, contributions by Apollinaire, and articles by Roch Grey, André Salmon, Paul Dermée, Francis Picabia, Pierre Albert-Birot, Henri Hertz, Ivan Goll, Alberto Savino and others. Excellent bibliography by Elie Richard, p[86–7].[32]

Additional special and commemorative issues are noted in Giedion-Welcker[8] and other bibliographies. See also the anthology published by Rimes et Raisons.[34]

Some French Readings

34. ADEMA, MARCEL, ed. Guillaume Apollinaire. Souvenirs et témoignages inédits de Louis de Gonzague Frick — Louise Faure-Favier — Roch Grey — Jeanne-Yves Blanc — Pierre Varenne — Jean Mollet — Pierre Albert-Birot — Albert Gleizes — Jean Metzinger — Léopold Survage, ré-unis et présentés par Marcel Adema. Supplément poétique. [94]p illus Albi, Editions de la Tête Noire, 1946.
"Cahier spécial de Rimes et Raisons." 70 numbered copies issued "sur velin blanc." Includes two unpublished pieces by Apollinaire.

35. AEGERTER, EMMANUEL et LABRACHERIE, PIERRE. Au temps de Guillaume. 241p Paris, Julliard, 1945.

36. APOLLINAIRE, GALERIE, LONDON. Apollinaire chez lui. [24]p illus London, Galerie Apollinaire, 1947.
"First exhibition under the patronage of Madame Jacqueline Apollinaire de Kostrowitzki." Booklet includes preface by André Billy, a translation of Apollinaire's "La Jolie Rousse" (Jacqueline Kolb) and among the plates three "Calligrammes." The final note by J. N. Schmitt acknowledges help for the exhibition "organized by Christine Givry." The gallery also issued a less pretentious catalog.[66]

37. BILLY, ANDRÉ. Apollinaire vivant. 119p illus Paris, Editions de la Sirène, 1923.
Includes Picasso portraits of Apollinaire.

38. BILLY, ANDRÉ. Guillaume Apollinaire. Une étude par André Billy; un choix de poèmes et une bibliographie établis par Henri Parisot, des inédits, des manuscrits, des dessins, des portraits. [246]p Paris, Pierre Seghers, 1947 (Poètes d'aujourd'hui. 8)

39. BRETON, ANDRÉ. Guillaume Apollinaire. *In his* Les Pas perdus. p25–45 Paris, N R F, Librairie Gallimard, 1924. (Les documents bleus, no6)
Essay dated "1917."

40. CADOU, RENÉ GUY. Le Testament d'Apollinaire: témoignage. Paris, 1945.

41. CARCO, FRANCIS. De Montmartre au Quartier Latin. p167–195 Paris, Edition du Nord, 1938.

42. FAURE-FAVRIER, LOUISE. Souvenirs sur Apollinaire. 242p Paris, Bernard Grasset, 1945.
Like the special issue of L'Esprit Nouveau,[33] this contains many interesting illustrations.

43. GREY, ROCH. Guillaume Apollinaire. Dessin d'Irène Lagut. Paris, Editions "SIC," 1918.

44. LALOU, RENÉ. Le cubisme et dada. *In his* Histoire de la littérature française contemporain. v2, p144–155 Paris, Presses Universitaires de France, 1940.
Revision of Crès edition (Paris, 1922), which was issued in an English translation (London, New York, 1924).

45. NADEAU, MAURICE. Les Poètes dans la guerre. *In his* Histoire du surréalism. p35–43 Paris, Editions du Seuil, 1945.

46. RAYMOND, MARCEL. De Baudelaire au surréalisme. p228–238 et passim. Paris, José Corti, 1947.
Revised edition of work first published by R. A. Corrêa, 1933, subtitled "Essai sur le mouvement poétique contemporain." (To be issued in translation by Wittenborn, Schultz, New York, 1949)

47. ROUVEYRE, ANDRÉ. Apollinaire. 268p illus Paris, Gallimard, 1945.
"Les divers chapitres de cet ouvrage ont paru dans les revues suivantes: Le Mercure de France, *Septembre 1920;* La N R F, *avril et mai, 1942;* Fontaine, *Alger, 1943;* Confluences, *novembre 1943."*

48. ROUVEYRE, ANDRÉ. Le culte de Guillaume Apollinaire. Arts et Métiers Graphiques no17, p1–8 May 15, 1930.
On the N R F édition de luxe of "Calligrammes" with two specimen pages from the press of Maurice Darantière.

49. SALMON, ANDRÉ. Vie de Guillaume Apollinaire. La Nouvelle Revue Française p675–693 Nov 1920.

50. SALMON, ANDRÉ. La Négresse du Sacré-Coeur. 237p Paris, Nouvelle Revue Française, 1920.
A novel of Montmartre which includes the Apollinaire circle. Also issued in translation as: The Black Venus. New York, Macaulay, 1929.[63]

51. SKIRA, ALBERT. Anthologie du livre illustré par les peintres et sculpteurs de l'école de Paris. nos50,81,95,99,101,106,124 Genève, Albert Skira, 1946.
A record of the fascination which Apollinaire's texts have exercised over distinguished publishers and imaginative artists, some of which, like the Derain L'Enchanteur pourrissant (1909) and the Dufy Le Bestaire (1919) form part of the pictorial achievements of his generation.

52. TOUSSAINT-LUCA, A. Guillaume Apollinaire (Souvenirs d'un ami). 50p Paris, Editions de la Phalange, 1920.

Some English Readings

53. BALAKIAN, ANNA. The road to the absolute. *In her* Literary origins of surrealism. p98–126 New York, King's Crown press, 1937.

54. BOWRA, C. M. Introduction. *In* Apollinaire, Guillaume. Choix de poésies. pvii–xvi London, Horizon, 1945.

55. DOUGLAS, CHARLES. Artist quarter, reminiscences of Montmartre and Montparnasse in the first two decades of the twentieth century. p56–64 et passim London, Faber and Faber, 1941.
An English counterpart to Carco.[41]

56. EUROPEAN CARAVAN. An anthology of the new spirit in European literature, compiled and edited by Samuel Putnam and others. p7–8,64–76 New York, Brewer, Warren & Putnam, 1931.
Includes translations from Calligrammes, *p65–76.*

57. LEMAITRE, GEORGES. From cubism to surrealism in French literature. p71–155 London, Oxford University press; Cambridge, Mass., Harvard University press, 1947.
The most adequate study of Apollinaire and his time in English, including bibliography. Revision of 1941 edition. The chapter on cubism includes an extensive discussion on Apollinaire, p93–121. Bibliography, p225 et passim. "Admirably detailed . . . though markedly hostile because middle-class in point of view" (Robert Motherwell[12])

58. MACKWORTH, CECILY. "Je suis Guillaume Apollinaire." Horizon v11, no62, p90–103 Feb 1945.
An excellent essay which, with Lemaitre[57] and Balakian,[53] constitutes a rounded survey of Apollinaire for English readers.

59. MESENS, E. L. T. Notes [on "Les Peintres cubistes"] p10,12,15 *In* London Gallery, Ltd. The cubist spirit in its time. London, 1947.
The author severely criticizes the inaccuracy and inadequacy of Apollinaire's views. See exhibition catalog.[110]

60. OSBORNE, LUCY EUGENIA. Carmina figurata & the Aldine Theocritus. The Colophon part 13, [8]p Spring 1930.
On "early shaped verse." There is "no little interest to find in an age in which conventions are being cast aside rather than rigidly followed that an author

[Apollinaire] would choose deliberately to revive an ancient artifice." An illuminating fragment on Apollinaire's erudition and classicism. Kahnweiler (p46)[89] *also discusses this pictorial device, and Rouveyre as well.*[48]

61. ROSENFELD, PAUL. Guillaume Apollinaire. *In his* Men seen, twenty-four modern authors. p65–85 New York, Lincoln Mac-Veagh, Dial press, 1925.

62. ROBSJOHN-GIBBINGS, T. H. L'Elite, c'est moi. *In his* Mona Lisa's mustache, a dissection of modern art. New York, Alfred A. Knopf, 1947.
A distorted attack on cubism, Apollinaire and others of his circle as "occult" and "esoteric aesthetics."

63. SALMON, ANDRÉ. The black Venus. (La Négresse de [!] Sacré Coeur). Translated from the French by Slater Brown. 293p New York, Macauley co., 1929.
See note on French edition.[50]

Exhibitions

64. DE BEAUNE, GALERIE, PARIS. Guillaume Apollinaire et ses peintres [Paris, 1938]
Announcement of exhibition held June 17, 1938, with preface by Jean Fraysse and list of painters represented.

65. BRETEAU, RENÉ. [Guillaume Apollinaire, exposition commémorative] Dec 1943.
"Luxueux catalogue qu'il [Breteau] édita [avec] Gaston Diehl." (Cited by Pierre Varenne in Rimes et Raisons[34]).

66. APOLLINAIRE, GALERIE, LONDON. Apollinaire chez lui. [London, 1947]
Catalog of exhibition held December 1947 which included 57 items by artists linked to Apollinaire. Nos. 1–14 consisted of water-colors and calligramme manuscripts by Apollinaire. See also exhibition booklet.[36]

Part 2: *The Movement*   *"Does the difficulty which even a sensible and cultivated public experiences in reading modern works result from present conditions? We will admit that it does; but it may be transformed into a source of enjoyment. . . . The transformation is extremely slow . . . for how should comprehension evolve as readily as the creative faculties? It follows in their wake."*   Albert Gleizes (1913)[69]

Among the *early* references on cubism are those by André Salmon,[67] a friend of Apollinaire, and the writings by the cubist painters Jean Metzinger and Albert Gleizes.[68-69] The book by the American collector Arthur Jerome Eddy[70] still holds its place as an enthusiastic and prophetic study, while the essays by critics of three nationalities, Coquiot,[71] Fechter,[72] and Soffici,[73] represent contemporary estimates of the cubists.

A selection of the extensive literature on cubism in French, German and English is noted in nos. 75–110. The most valuable works for the American reader are those by Barr[108] and Ozenfant.[102]

However, no serious study of the movement can be considered complete without the historical surveys by Einstein,[94] Huyghe[83] and Wilenski,[106] the accounts based on the intimate knowledge of perspicacious dealers like Kahnweiler[89] and Rosenberg,[75] as well as the analytical statements by Janneau[80] and Sweeney.[105] For an extensive bibliography, consult the compilation by Bazin;[82] for a general chronology consult Cogniat.[107]

Reproductions of the cubist painters and their creations in other media can be most conveniently examined in Barr,[108] Bonfante,[14a] Einstein,[94] Huyghe,[83, 99] and Zervos.[85] Among periodicals with similar coverage are *Bulletin de l'Effort Moderne,*[75] *L'Esprit Nouveau,*[77] and *Cahiers d'Art,*[76] which in its early years concerned itself, in large measure, with the work of Braque, Picasso, Léger and other cubists.

The exhibitions held at Paris (1935),[107] New York (1936),[108] Paris (1945)[109] and London (1947)[110] for which important catalogs were issued, indicate the continued interest in cubism which has not abated since the demise of its brilliant spokesman. "Apollinaire was the personification of cubism, and cubism was undoubtedly one of the turning points in the spiritual history of Europe."[58]

Early Works on Cubism

67. SALMON, ANDRÉ. Histoire anecdotique du cubisme. *In his* La Jeune peinture française. p41–61 Paris, Société des Trente, Albert Messein, 1912.

68. GLEIZES, ALBERT *et* METZINGER, JEAN. Du "Cubisme." 44p plus 24 illus Paris, Eugène Figuière, 1912 (Collection Tous les arts).
Apollinaire refers to Metzinger as "le premier théoricien du cubisme." Gleizes has also written: Du Cubisme. (Genève, 1918) — Du Cubisme et des moyens de le comprendre. (Paris, La Cible, 1920) — La Peinture et ses lois. Ce qui devait sortir du cubisme. (Paris, 1924. Published Mar 1923 in "La Vie des Lettres et des Arts") — Cubisme. Vers une conscience plastique, essai de généralisation (Munich, Albert Langen, 1925) — Tradition et cubisme. Articles et conférences 1912–1924 (Paris, La Cible, Chez J. Povolozky, 1927) — Kubismus (München, Langen, 1928)[93]

69. GLEIZES, ALBERT *and* METZINGER, JEAN. Cubism. (Translated). 133p incl illus London, Leipsic, T. Fisher Unwin, 1913.
"First English edition" of 1912 work. Text, 64p — Illustrations, 25 plates.

70. EDDY, ARTHUR JEROME. Cubists and post-impressionism. p60–109 illus (some colored) Chicago, McClurg, 1914.
"What is cubism," p60–89. — "The theory of cubism," p90–109. — Bibliography. Written 1913, revised edition issued 1919.

71. COQUIOT, GUSTAVE. Cubistes, futuristes, passéistes; essai sur la jeune peinture et la jeune sculpture. 3e éd 277p illus Paris, Ollendorff, 1914.
First edition included 48 reproductions. The new edition in 1923 had 24 reproductions "hors-texte," modified pagination, omitted some and added other artists.

72. FECHTER, PAUL. Der Kubismus. *In his* Der Expressionismus. p30–41 illus München, Piper, 1914.

73. SOFFICI, ARDENGO. Cubismo e futurismo. 2a ed 78p illus. Firenze, Libreria della Voce, 1914.
Further impressions on cubism and Apollinaire were incorporated in his: Ricordi di vita artistica e letteraria. Florence, Vallecchi, 1942 (c1930).

74. LAFORA, G. R. Estudio psicológico del cubismo y expresionismo. 37 illus. Archivos de Neurofiologia (Madrid) v3, no2, p1–37 plus plates June 1922.
Possibly the earliest study of cubism from this viewpoint. Includes an analysis of Apollinaire's "Les Peintres cubistes," p6 seq (Copy in Metropolitan Museum Library, New York).

Cubism: Selected References in French

75. Bulletin de "L'Effort Moderne." Directeur: Léonce Rosenberg. No1–40, Jan 1924–Dec 1927.
An illustrated journal issued by the Galerie "L'Effort Moderne" which handled cubist artists, and in its bulletin published many articles on as well as by the cubists painters. Essays also issued as separate pamphlets and reprinted in other magazines.

76. Cahiers d'Art. Edited by Christian Zervos. Paris, 1926 — current.
A major archive on modern art, which in its early years rallied to cubism and such artists as Braque, Gris, Picasso. The editor has also issued separate monographs based on material published in this encyclopedic periodical, as well as a pictorial anthology.[85]

77. L'Esprit Nouveau. Edited by Le Corbusier and A. Ozenfant. Paris, 1920–1925.
Vigorous propaganda for "the new spirit" in the contemporary arts which was the source of subsequent publications,[78–79] and the special issue on Apollinaire.[33]

78. OZENFANT, AMEDÉE *et* JEANNERET, CHARLES ÉDOUARD. La Peinture moderne. 172p illus Paris, G. Crès, 1925. (Collection de l'Esprit nouveau)
Includes essays from L'Esprit Nouveau on cubism, p89–131.

79. OZENFANT, AMEDÉE. Le Cubisme. *In his* Art. 6e éd p51–88 Paris, Jean Budry, 1929.
Translated as: Foundations of modern art. New York, Brewer, Warren & Putnam, 1931.[102] — Leben und Gestaltung. Potsdam, 1930.[95]

80. JANNEAU, GUILLAUME. L'Art cubiste. Théories et réalisations, étude critique. 111p 48 illus (some colored) Paris, Charles Moreau, 1929.

Contents: I. Les origines et les premiers essais. — II. La formation de l'école. — III. La doctrine. — IV. L'école de la peinture pure. — V. Le cubisme expressioniste. — VI. Conséquences et position du cubisme.

81. PUY, MICHEL. Les Assises du cubisme. *In his* L'Effort des peintres modernes. p129–158 Paris, Messein, 1933.
Deals with the 1911–1914 period. Part IV, p142–146, reviews "Les Peintres cubistes" and Apollinaire.

82. BAZIN, GERMAIN. Historique du cubisme. L'Amour de l'Art v14, no9, p219–20 Nov 1933.
Condensed survey and extensive bibliography (p220). Quotes brief text of Gil Blas *(Nov 14 1908) where term* des cubes *— based upon an observation by Matisse — was first introduced into print by Louis Vauxcelles. Reprinted in Huyghe.*[83]

83. HUYGHE, RENÉ, *ed.* Le Cubisme. *In his* Histoire de l'art contemporain: la peinture. p209–238. Paris, Alcan, 1935.
Contents: Introduction par René Huyghe, p209–214 — Naissance du cubisme, par André Lhote, p215–218. — Notices: Historique du cubisme, Bibliographie générale, p219–220, par Germain Bazin. — Le Cubisme lyrique. 1. Pablo Picasso, par Germain Bazin, p221–225. — Notices, p225–6. — II. Braque, Marcoussis et Juan Gris, par Jean Cassou, p227–31. — Notices, p232–3. — Le Cubisme méthodique: Léger et "l'effort moderne," par Raymond Cogniat, p234–36. — Notices, p236–38. "Les notices de ce chapitre ont été établies par Germain Bazin." Originally published in L'Amour de l'Art Nov 1933.

84. ESCHOLIER, RAYMOND. Le Cubisme. *In his* La Peinture française, XXe siècle. p72–103 illus Paris, Librairie Floury, 1937.

85. ZERVOS, CHRISTIAN. Histoire de l'art contemporain. p193–310 Paris, Cahiers d'Art, 1938.
The following sections include brief text and numerous plates: Le Cubisme, p193–248. — Epanouissement du cubisme, p249–296. — La Sculpture cubiste, p297–310. See also Cahiers d'Art.[76]

86. HUYGHE, RENÉ. Le cubisme et ses développements. *In his* La Peinture française: les contemporains. p31–39, plates 67–124 (some colored) Paris, Pierre Tisné, 1939.

Also issued in English text as "French painting: the contemporaries."[99]

87. DORIVAL, BERNARD. Le Fauvisme et le cubisme (1905–1911). 361p Paris, N R F, Gallimard, 1944. (Les Etapes de la peinture française contemporaine. Tome II)
Bibliography, p347–359.

88. FRANCASTEL, PIERRE. Les Maîtres de l'art contemporain: le cubisme. *In his* Nouveau dessin, nouvelle peinture: l'école de Paris. p113–154 illus Paris, Librairie de Médicis, 1946.

89. KAHNWEILER, DANIEL-HENRY. Juan Gris, his life and work. Translated by Douglas Cooper. 166p plus plates London, Lund Humphries, 1947.
A translation of: Juan Gris, sa vie, son oeuvre, ses écrits *(344p illus Paris, Gallimard, 1947) the text of which has been "adapted" and expanded by the translator, "particularly in part III" (appendices). Important sections are "The birth of cubism" (p69–78) and specific commentary on Apollinaire (p46,124–125) but there are numerous references to the poet and critic, as well as the movement and its practitioners, that illuminate the intellectual and artistic circles of Paris in its cubist days. This able art-dealer points out that the reference to Apollinaire as "the moving spirit of cubism . . . is not so much an error as a distortion of historical fact."*

Cubism: Selected References in German

90. KAHNWEILER, DANIEL-HENRY. Der Weg zum Kubismus. Mit 47 Zinkätzungen und 6 Gravüren. 55p. München, Delphin-Verlag, 1920.
A review emphasizng the role of Picasso, Braque and Léger. Issued in translation as The rise of cubism, New York, Wittenborn, Schultz, inc., 1949.[99a]

91. KÜPPERS, PAUL ERICH. Der Kubismus, ein künstlerisches Formproblem unserer Zeit. 62p plus 40 illus Leipzig, Klinkhardt & Biermann, 1920.
Includes bibliography of works dated 1911–1920, and international list of periodicals.

92. BLÜMNER, RUDOLF. Der Geist des Kubismus und die Künste. 69p illus Berlin, Der Sturm, 1921.

93. GLEIZES, ALBERT. Kubismus. 101p incl 47 illus München, Albert Langen, 1928 (Bauhausbücher 13)
Contents: I. Geschichte des Kubismus (1928), p7–31 — Abbildungen 1–47, p34–80. II. Kubismus, ein neues Formgewissen, Versuch einer Verallgemeinerung (1926), p82–101. The plates are annotated.

94. EINSTEIN, CARL. Der Kubismus. *In his* Die Kunst des 20. Jahrhunderts. 2. Aufl. p55–100,262–335. Berlin, Propyläen-Verlag, 1928 (c1926)
A survey stressing Picasso, Braque, Gris, Léger. Pages 262–335 are plates, some colored.

95. OZENFANT, AMEDÉE. Leben und Gestaltung, 316p Potsdam, Müller & Kiepenheuer, 1930.
A translation of his Art *(1929).*[79]

Cubism: Selected References in English

96. CHARLOT, JEAN. Cubism: requiescat in pace. *In his* Art from the Mayans to Disney. p193–218 New York, London, Sheed and Ward, 1939.
Originally published in American Scholar v8 p102–114 1938. Charlot and Paalen[103] *represent the views of two contemporary painters.*

97. GIEDION, SIGFRIED. The research into space: cubism. *In his* Space, time and architecture, the growth of a new tradition. p355–363. Cambridge, Harvard University press, 1941.

98. GORDON, JAN. Cubism. *In his* Modern French painters. p132–149 illus New York, Dodd, Mead, 1923.
The English estimate of the movement is represented by two critics, Gordon and Read.[104]

99. HUYGHE, RENÉ. Cubism and its development. *In his* French painting: the contemporaries. p31–39, plates 67–92 (some colored) New York, French and European publications, 1939.
Translation of "La Peinture française."[86]

99a. KAHNWEILER, DANIEL-HENRY. The rise of cubism. Translated by Henry Aronson. illus New York, Wittenborn, Schultz, inc., 1949. (The documents of modern art, edited by Robert Motherwell)
A translation of Der Weg zum Kubismus.[90]

100. MOHOLY-NAGY, LASZLO. Cubism. *In his* Vision in motion. p116–140 illus Chicago, Paul Theobald, 1947.

101. NEW YORK, MUSEUM OF MODERN ART. Cubism and abstract art by Alfred H. Barr, Jr. New York, 1936.
See notes under exhibitions.[108]

102. OZENFANT, AMEDÉE. Foundations of modern art. p43–83 illus New York, Brewer, Warren & Putnam, London, John Rodker, 1931.
Translation by John Rodker of his Art *(1929).*[79] *"From before the flood to 1914. Cubism." p43–83. The author, who speaks with special competence as an independent artist and editor of L'Esprit Nouveau,*[77] *reserves cubism as a term for works painted earlier than 1914. Later chapters ("Picassoism 1914–1928," "Painting 1914–1918") deal with other artists mentioned by Apollinaire.*

103. PAALEN, WOLFGANG. On the meaning of cubism today. *In his* Form and sense. p23–30 illus New York, Wittenborn, 1945 (Problems of contemporary art)
Originally published in Dyn vi, no6 p4–8 Nov 1944.

104. READ, HERBERT. Art now, an introduction to the theory of modern painting and sculpture. p96–104 illus London, Faber and Faber, 1948.
Revision of 1933 and 1936 editions.

105. SWEENEY, JAMES JOHNSON. From this side of cubism. *In his* Plastic redirections in 20th century painting. p39–64 incl illus Chicago, University of Chicago press, 1934.

106. WILENSKI, REGINALD HOWARD. Modern French painters. 424p illus New York, Reynal & Hitchcock, 1944 (c1940).
A chronological survey of contemporary art, with special emphasis on the historical milieu. Material on Apollinaire, cubism and its associated artists is most conveniently localized by the detailed index. Bibliographical references.

63

Exhibitions

107. LA GAZETTE DES BEAUX-ARTS, PARIS. Les Créateurs du cubisme, mars–avril 1935. Préface de Maurice Raynal, catalogue par Raymond Cogniat. 2ᵉ éd 32p illus Paris, 1935. (Les Etapes de l'art contemporain. V)
"Les catalogues des expositions de Beaux-Arts et de la Gazette des Beaux-Arts, no13." Includes essay "Le Cubisme" by Raynal and valuable "Notes chronologiques" (1881–1918) by Cogniat, as well as illustrations, catalog and biographical data.

108. NEW YORK, MUSEUM OF MODERN ART. Cubism and abstract art. 249p incl illus New York, Museum of Modern Art, 1936.
An historical survey of abstract and cubist art in Europe, organized and analyzed by Alfred H. Barr, Jr. This authority devotes three sections of text and plates to "analytical cubism" (p29–53), "synthetic cubism" (p77–102) and "cubist sculpture" (p103–115). Includes valuable chronologies, extensive catalog and bibliography.

109. GALERIE DE FRANCE, PARIS. Le Cubisme, 1911–1918. G. Braque, R. Delaunay, R. de La Fresnaye, A. Gleizes, J. Gris, A. Herbin, F. Léger, A. Lhote, L. Marcoussis, J. Metzinger, P. Picasso, J. Villon, 60p illus Paris, Galerie de France, 1945.
Exhibition of 50 paintings, held May 25–June 30. "Le Cubisme" by Bernard Dorival, p5–20. — Notices biographiques, p21–30. — "Planches et commentaires" by André Lhote, p35–59.

110. LONDON GALLERY, LTD., LONDON. The cubist spirit in its time, 18 March–3 May 1947. 39p illus London, London Gallery, ltd., 1947.
Exhibition organized by E. L. T. Mesens, catalog compiled by Robert Melville and E. L. T. Mesens. "Birth and christening of cubism as recorded in Les Peintres Cubistes by Guillaume Apollinaire," p8. — "Notes" by Mesens (p10,12,15) severely criticize Apollinaire's views. The chronological catalog contains illuminating illustrations. Extracts from André Breton on cubism, Braque and Duchamp (p34–36,39).

Alphabetical Index to Bibliography